SEAFOOD COOK BOOK

By the Editors of Sunset Magazine
and Sunset Books

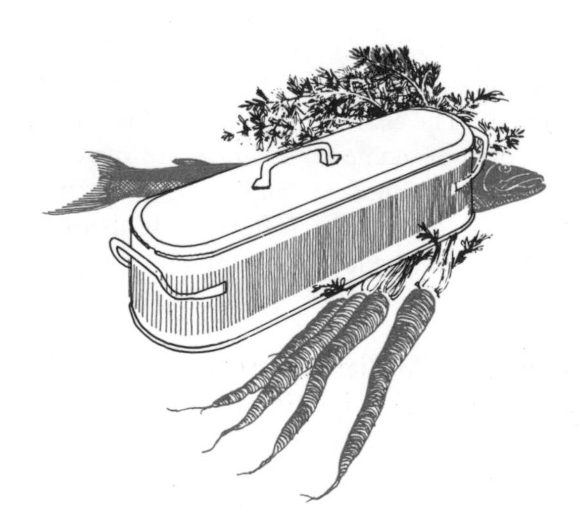

Lane Books · Menlo Park, California

ABOUT THIS BOOK

Master the art of fish cookery and it will open up a wide world of new dishes to serve your family and guests. Some of the simplest and quickest cooking methods give the finest results with fish; for this reason alone, it deserves more attention in today's meal planning.

This book aims to show how simple it is to become an expert with fish and shellfish. Chapter by chapter, it is organized to eliminate confusion about names of fish and to help you buy with confidence. It emphasizes the similarities of fish varieties and shows how recipes and cooking methods can be interchanged. It is tailored to the fish and shellfish from the Pacific Coast.

The twenty most important fish sold in our markets are actually called by more than sixty different names. You see all of their names in the chart on pages 12-13; notice the number of times such names as sea bass, cod, and perch reappear.

This situation confuses the fish dealer, as well as the shopper, and many cooks simply retreat from the confusion and buy a limited few fish they know and recognize, like salmon, swordfish, or sole. In doing so, they miss a wide spectrum of other delicious and plentiful fish.

The buying guide chart on pages 12-13, used with the illustrations of market fish on that page, can help you to identify the fish you buy. The chart lists first the officially recognized common name (by general agreement of Federal, state, and university scientists in the fisheries field); then, in parentheses, those names are listed by which the same fish may be known in different localities or even in neighboring fish markets within the same locality. (Rockfish and sablefish, for example, are almost never called by their official names in fish markets.) Best advice: If the fish dealer doesn't seem to recognize one name, try another.

Most of the whitish looking fillets you see in fish markets can be classified as very lean and mild in flavor; recipes for their use are often interchangeable and have been grouped in one chapter of this book. A group of market fish that are either fatter or more pronounced in flavor (or both fatter and more flavorful) are described in another chapter. All of these fish are unique in one way or another and require some special handling for best results.

For purposes of helping the cook decide how to cook them, all the small whole fish are grouped in a separate chapter. Two very popular fish choices—lean, mild sole and fat, rich salmon—also have separate chapters devoted to their varied recipes. A final fish chapter deals with sportfish, and explains how to do the jobs of cleaning, skinning, and filleting, work usually done for you when you buy fish in the market.

The second part of the book deals with shellfish. These chapters offer many ideas for ways to cook and serve the convenient forms in which most shellfish are available. Certain shellfish (mussels and clams, for example) may require that you first catch or dig them, so these chapters also include information on cleaning and caring for the catch.

Cover photograph by Glenn M. Christiansen; recipe on page 75, Shellfish Cioppino.
Illustrations by Richard Garrett.

Third Printing October 1968

 Library of Congress Catalog Card Number 67-12506. Title Number 258. Lithographed in U.S.A.

CONTENTS

BE AN EXPERT WITH FISH 4

Buying Guide for Pacific Fish • Basic Cooking Techniques • Fish Sauces • How to Freeze Fish

SOLE 14

Small Boneless Fillets • Lean, White, Mild-Flavored • Buying Guide • Varieties Available • Quick Sauté Dishes • Make-Ahead Baked Dishes

LEAN, MILD FISH 20

Halibut • Rockfish • Lingcod • Pacific Cod • Seabass • Similarities of Lean, Mild Fish • Substituting Them in Recipes • Cooking Methods

SALMON 28

Fresh • Kippered • Seasons • Buying Guide • Salmon on the Barbecue • Cooking Whole Salmon, Steaks and Fillets

UNIQUE AND FATTER FISH 35

Barracuda • Sablefish • Shad • Sturgeon • Swordfish • Albacore • Seasons • Buying Guides • Characteristics of Each Fish • Cooking Methods • Barbecue Sauces

PAN-SIZED WHOLE FISH 46

Mackerel • Smelt • Surfperch • Trout • Description of Each Fish • Buying Guides • Cooking Methods

SPORTSMAN'S CATCH 51

Bonito • Sheepshead • Kelp Bass • Sand Bass • Striped Bass • Cleaning • Scaling • Trimming • Skinning Cutting Steaks • Filleting • Skinning Fillets • Cooking Methods

SHRIMP 57

Fresh • Frozen • Canned • Deveining • Cooking • Substituting Different Forms in Recipes

LOBSTER 64

Spiny Pacific and Northeastern Lobsters • Preparing and Serving Live Lobsters, Frozen Lobster Tails, Precooked Lobsters

CRAB 71

Dungeness Crab • Alaska King Crab • Buying Guides • Cleaning, Cracking, and Cooking Live Dungeness Crab • Serving Cracked Dungeness Crab • Sauces • King Crab on the Half Shell

OYSTERS AND SCALLOPS 79

Pacific, Olympia, and Eastern Oysters • Frozen Scallops • Buying Guides • Cooking Methods

CLAMS, MUSSELS, ABALONE 87

Clam Varieties • Gathering • Shucking • Buying Guides • Cooking Methods

BE AN EXPERT WITH FISH

Six Basic Cooking Methods

Despite the wealth of fine fresh fish available, fish cookery is probably the least well understood and most frequently abused form of cookery in our homes and restaurants.

By nature fish is tender and free of tough fibers that need to be softened by cooking. The result of cooking it is much the same as when you cook an egg; heat firms the delicate protein. Like an egg, fish becomes tough and dry when overcooked.

Recognizing when fish is done is the first step in learning to cook it well. Recipes usually tell you to cook fish until it flakes when tested with a fork. The close-up drawing on page 5 illustrates what it means to cook until the fish flakes. In this drawing of an especially loose textured fish, you can see the way the flesh slides apart in its natural divisions when done; once observed, it is easy to recognize when any fish is done. If you cook a whole fish or large piece of fish, probe into the center of the thickest part to test for doneness.

Much of the know-how about fish cookery can be simplified to a set of step-by-step directions for each of six basic cooking techniques. These techniques will be described in the pages that follow. They will enable you to prepare serving-sized pieces of almost any fish in the markets.

The chart on pages 12-13 indicates the fat content of each fish; this is one important clue to the best way to cook it. In general, fish with higher amounts of fat are preferred for broiling, barbecuing, and baking; their natural fat helps keep them moist as they cook. Lean fish are somewhat easier to poach, for their flesh usually firms as it cooks and does not fall apart as easily as that of fat fish. But any one of these basic cooking methods is applicable to many different fish (sometimes with allowances for fat content), making possible an extensive repertory of fish dishes without the addition of a single other recipe.

Your decision about which cooking method to use for the fish you have will depend partly on the fish variety and its size and shape, but the cooking method also depends on your menu. Frequently, cooking fish is a last minute job. If you are serving sole fillets, for example, it is a good idea to have the family all seated at the table and the rest of the dinner ready before slipping the fish into a hot pan for its one-minute-on-each-side browning.

Other fish may take a little longer than sole to sauté, broil, barbecue, or fry, but you will usually want to have the rest of the meal ready before you start to cook the fish by one of these methods.

Not all fish cookery must be done at the last minute. Any fish, even sole fillets, can be adapted to make-ahead dishes that cook unattended in the oven. You'll find examples of this kind of fish cookery in every chapter of this book, including many dishes that are good choices for company dinners.

BUTTER-SAUTÉING

Butter-sautéing is one of the easiest and quickest of all ways to cook fish. The French term for this cooking method is *à la meuniere*. Fine restaurants frequently cook fish and shellfish this way, but it is too often overlooked for meals at home.

You can use this method for any thin fish fillets or steaks, or for small, whole fish such as trout or smelt. Whether the fish is fat or lean makes little difference. Butter, salt, and pepper are the only seasonings needed, and they enhance the natural flavor of the fish, pronounced or mild. Of course, the freshest possible fish gives the best results.

You will need a good frying pan that distributes the heat evenly. The fish cooks in a small amount of fat and butter is preferred for flavor, but it does burn easily. A combination of half butter and half salad oil is easier to handle than all butter.

If you are willing to go to a little trouble to prepare some clarified butter, it burns less easily. To make clarified butter, put some butter in a pan; set it over the lowest heat on your range for about one hour. When you see that it has separated into clear butter on top with a milky residue beneath, carefully skim off the pure butter and strain it through four layers of cheesecloth that have been wrung out in cold water. You can do a whole pound of butter at one time and keep it in a covered dish in your refrigerator to use for browning fish and meat.

When well done, butter-sautéed fish has a very thin, crisp, golden coating over meltingly tender flesh. It may be served with a lemon butter sauce (recipe follows), if you wish.

HOW TO BUTTER SAUTÉ

1) Cut fish steaks or fillets into serving-sized pieces; they should be no more than about ⅝ inch thick. Clean small, whole fish; remove heads, if you wish. Wipe fish with a damp cloth.

2) In a frying pan (large enough so fish won't be crowded), heat about ⅛ inch of clarified butter, regular butter, or half butter and half salad oil.

3) Sprinkle fish pieces with salt and pepper; then dip in flour to lightly coat both sides.

4) Sauté over medium-high heat until browned; turn and brown the other side. The time required is about 1 minute per side for thin sole fillets, to about 3 minutes on a side for medium-sized trout.

5) Transfer to a warm plate and serve immediately. You might sprinkle the fish with chopped parsley or pour lemon butter sauce (recipe follows) over the fish on the serving plate.

LEMON BUTTER SAUCE:

As soon as you remove the fish from the frying pan, add a little additional butter to the pan (about 1 tablespoon for each 2 servings); heat until it browns lightly. Squeeze a few drops of lemon juice for each serving; then pour over the fish.

BROILING AND BARBECUING

Almost any fish may be broiled, but fish with very low fat content require a little different handling. Moderately fat and full-flavored fish, such as salmon, trout, and albacore, are best for the barbecue because the smoke enhances their flavor; smoke might overpower a delicately flavored fish. Fairly thick fish steaks or fillets may be placed directly on the greased grill of your barbecue, but smaller fish pieces are easier to handle and turn if held inside a hinged wire broiler.

Directions here will be for broiling and barbecuing serving-sized fish steaks or fillets and small, whole fish. Larger fish and whole fish fillets are very satisfactorily barbecued also, but require special instructions; look for these directions indexed under the name of the fish you wish to barbecue.

While broiling or barbecuing, the fish is basted with melted butter or a basting sauce. Some simple bastes are included here; others are given with specific fish recipes throughout the book.

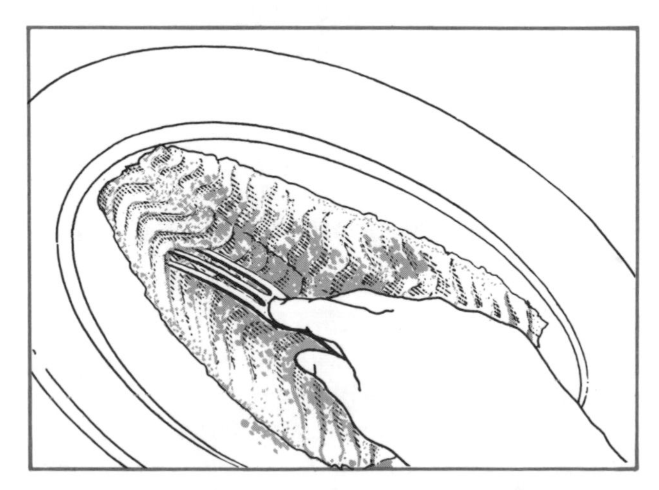

To tell when a fish is done, probe into thickest part with fork; flesh should slide into natural divisions.

HOW TO OVEN-BROIL FISH (EXCEPT THOSE WITH VERY LOW FAT)

1) Cut fish steaks or fillets in serving-sized pieces. Clean small, whole fish and remove the heads, if you wish. Wipe with a damp cloth.

2) Sprinkle both sides of fish lightly with salt and pepper.

3) Arrange fish pieces on a preheated greased broiler pan. Brush with melted butter; equal parts melted butter and lemon juice; or with equal parts melted butter, lemon juice, and dry sherry or vermouth. Broil 2 to 4 inches from the source of heat (put thicker pieces farther from heat) until lightly browned and the fish flakes when tested with a fork. Fillets are broiled on just one side; steaks should be turned, basted, then broiled on the other side until browned. Total broiling time is about 4 to 15 minutes, depending on thickness.

4) Remove to a warm serving plate and serve immediately.

HOW TO OVEN-BROIL VERY LEAN FISH

1) Prepare same as for fatter fish (see above).

2) After sprinkling with salt and pepper, dust lightly on both sides with flour.

3) Follow directions as for fatter fish, except drizzle the flour-dusted pieces generously with melted butter instead of brushing with butter or basting sauce.

HOW TO BARBECUE FISH

1) Cut fish into serving-sized steaks or fillets; they should be at least ½ inch thick. Clean small, whole fish and remove heads, if you wish. Wipe with a damp cloth.

2) Place the fish on a greased grill or hinged broiler over moderately hot coals. Baste with melted butter; with equal parts melted butter and lemon juice; or with equal parts melted butter, lemon juice, and dry sherry or vermouth. Grill, turning once, and basting often until the fish is browned and flakes when tested with a fork; time will be about 8 to 16 minutes, depending on thickness. Sprinkle with salt and pepper to taste.

3) Remove to a warm plate and serve at once.

POACHING

When you want to have some cooked fish to use for salad or sandwiches, or to serve as a cold entrée for a summer day, first poach the fish. Poaching means to simmer fish gently in a flavorful liquid. Any fish cooked this way is also delicious served hot with a fish sauce.

All the fish with very low fat content are especially satisfactory when cooked by this method. In addition, some of the more mildly flavored of the fatter fish, notably salmon, are fine for poaching. To poach a steak, fillet, or small chunk of fish, you need only a length of cheesecloth and a frying pan or other pan large enough to immerse the pieces in simmering liquid. Poaching may be done on top of the range or in the oven.

Imported kitchenwares shops sell special pans for poaching fish; they come in a wide range of sizes, all long and oval to fit a whole fish (such as salmon) and with a basket for lowering and raising the fish from the liquid. If you do not have a large fish poaching pan, there are ways to improvise with what you have; see How to Poach Salmon, on page 29.

The basic and simple poaching liquid given here is designed to point up the flavor of fish, but not to mask its natural flavor. The stock that remains after the fish is cooked can be the base of a flavorful sauce to serve with the fish (see pages 8-9).

BASIC POACHING LIQUID:

About 1 quart water
1 onion, sliced
6 whole black peppers
2 whole allspice
3 tablespoons lemon juice or white wine vinegar
1 bay leaf
1 teaspoon salt
½ cup dry white table wine (optional)

Combine all the ingredients in a pan. You will need enough to just cover the fish pieces, so the amount of water may be varied accordingly. The recipe may be doubled or tripled if larger amounts are needed. Simmer ingredients together for at least 20 minutes.

HOW TO POACH FISH

1) Wipe the fish pieces with a damp cloth.

2) If the fish is to be oven poached, wrap pieces in cheesecloth and arrange in a greased baking pan. When poaching on top of the range, wrap the pieces in cheesecloth or set the fish on a heat-proof plate and overwrap with cheesecloth.

3) Bring the basic poaching liquid (see above) to boiling and pour over the fish in the baking pan, or lower cheesecloth wrapped fish into simmering liquid.

4) Cover baking pan and put into a hot oven (425°), or reduce heat, cover pan, and simmer (water should never boil). Cook until the fish flakes when tested with a fork; start testing serving-sized pieces in about 6 minutes.

5) Lift cooked fish from the liquid with a wide spatula, supporting it with the cheesecloth, if necessary. Drain well; then unwrap and serve hot, or cool and chill. Serve with a fish sauce (see recipes on pages 8-11).

OVEN-FRYING

This method of crisply browning fish in the oven is similar to oven-frying chicken and offers some of the same advantages. It is quick, requires little attention, and there is no spattering of fat. Serving-sized steaks or fillets of fish or small whole fish may be cooked this way.

HOW TO OVEN-FRY FISH

1) Cut the fish in serving-sized pieces and wipe with a damp cloth.

2) Melt 2 to 4 tablespoons butter or margarine in a shallow baking pan either over direct heat or in the preheating oven (butter should generously coat the bottom of the pan).

3) Dip each piece of fish in milk; drain briefly. Sprinkle with salt and pepper; then roll in fine dry bread crumbs or cracker crumbs to coat all over.

4) Turn the crumb-coated fish over in the melted butter and arrange without crowding in the pan.

5) Bake on the top shelf of a very hot oven (500°) for 8 to 15 minutes, or until the fish flakes when tested with a fork. Turn once, if needed, to brown evenly on both sides. Serve immediately.

FRYING

Some diners prefer a thicker, crustier coating on cooked fish than that which results from butter-sautéing or oven-frying. This is achieved by dipping the fish in beaten egg and then in crumbs before frying it.

The frying can be done in deep or shallow fat. If you deep-fry fish, a thermometer will help you achieve the best temperature for browning with the least fat absorption.

Serving-sized (and smaller) portions of fish or pan-dressed small whole fish are suitable for frying.

HOW TO FRY OR DEEP-FRY FISH

1) Cut the fish in serving-sized pieces and wipe with a damp cloth.

2) Sprinkle both sides with salt and pepper.

3) For 4 to 6 servings of fish, beat 1 egg slightly and beat in 1 tablespoon milk. Have ready about 1 cup fine dry bread crumbs, cracker crumbs, or a prepared coating mix.

4) Dip each piece of fish in the egg mixture to coat all over; drain briefly; then roll in the crumbs to coat both sides evenly.

5) In a heavy frying pan, heat about 1/8 inch shortening or salad oil over moderately high heat. If you prefer to use a deep-fat fryer, heat shortening or salad oil (enough to cover the fish — pan should not be over 1/2 full) to 375°.

6) Place fish in a frying pan without crowding, or lower the fish in a frying basket into deep fat. Fry in the pan until brown on one side; turn carefully and brown the other side. When fish is golden brown and flakes when tested with a fork, remove and drain on paper towels. Cooking time will be about 5 to 10 minutes if done in a frying pan, about 3 to 5 minutes in deep fat, but varies according to thickness of fish. Serve immediately.

FISH SAUCES

A sauce often makes the difference between an ordinary serving of fish and the kind of fish dish you might enjoy at a fine restaurant. Fresh fish, well cooked, then served with an appropriate sauce, is something you can offer with pride to your most discriminating guests.

Many of the finest sauces are easy to make, and others can be greatly simplified by using an electric blender. Included here are several types of fish sauces, with suggestions for the fish they best complement. Other sauces are included with recipes for specific fish and shellfish.

HOLLANDAISE SAUCES

In these two sauces, you make Hollandaise in an electric blender, then stir in flavoring ingredients.

Serve Hollandaise sauces warm, or rewarm them, stirring over hot (not boiling) water.

Sauce Hollandaise with Cucumber (for salmon, halibut, trout, albacore)

Combine in the blender 3 egg yolks (at room temperature) and 1 1/2 tablespoons lemon juice. Melt 3/4 cup butter or margarine and heat until it bubbles; don't brown. Add 1 tablespoon hot water to the egg; turn blender on high speed and immediately pour in hot butter in a steady stream (takes about 5 seconds). Add 1 teaspoon prepared mustard and 1/2 teaspoon salt; whirl until blended, about 30 seconds. Turn into a bowl and stir in 1 tablespoon chopped parsley and 1 tablespoon chopped chives. Peel 1 cucumber; cut in half and scrape out large seeds; chop and stir into sauce. Makes about 2 cups.

Sauce Hollandaise with Shrimp (for salmon, sole, halibut, sea bass, rockfish)

Prepare as for Hollandaise above, but omit salt; turn into a bowl; omit cucumber and stir in 1 can (about 5 oz.) shrimp, rinsed and drained.

FISH STOCK SAUCES

The thickened fish stock (fish velouté in classic cooking terms) is the base of many fine fish sauces. It is especially suitable to use for poached fish, since you can use the poaching liquid for the fish stock.

You can make fish stock to have on hand and even freeze it in small amounts for use in making sauces or as a fish poaching liquid.

FISH STOCK (FUMET DE POISSON):

2 tablespoons butter or margarine
1 cup minced onion
1 cup minced parsley
4 pounds fish bones, trimmings, and heads (preferably sole or any other white fish)
3 tablespoons lemon juice
1½ cups dry white wine
2 quarts cold water

Melt butter in a large pan and sauté the onions and parsley just until wilted. Lay the fish bones over these; add the lemon juice and cook over low heat, shaking occasionally, for 5 minutes. Add the wine and simmer, uncovered, until the liquid is reduced one half, about 20 to 30 minutes. Then add the water; bring to the boiling point and boil rapidly for 30 minutes or until reduced by half; strain. Makes 4 cups. Freeze in small amounts.

Fish Velouté Sauce (for any fish)

Melt 3 tablespoons butter or margarine in a pan. Stir in 3 tablespoons flour and cook until bubbly. Remove from heat and gradually stir in 2 cups fish stock (see above), or basic poaching liquid (see page 7). Continue cooking, stirring, until thickened. Add salt and pepper if needed, and a dash nutmeg. Sprinkle with some finely chopped parsley if you wish.

Bercy Sauce (for halibut, rockfish, trout)

Prepare as for fish velouté sauce above, except sauté 2 chopped shallots or green onions and 1 tablespoon chopped parsley in the melted butter before adding the flour. Use only 1½ cups fish stock and add ½ cup dry white wine.

Estragon Sauce (for rockfish, halibut, sole, salmon)

Make fish velouté sauce as directed above, stirring ¼ teaspoon tarragon into the butter with the flour. Use 1½ cups fish stock with ½ cup heavy cream.

Mornay Sauce (for halibut, sole, rockfish)

Prepare fish velouté sauce as directed above, using only 2 tablespoons flour. Use 1½ cups fish stock and ½ cup light cream. When thickened, stir in ¾ cup shredded Gruyere or Swiss cheese and ¼ cup grated Parmesan; continue cooking over low heat just until cheese has melted.

Curry Sauce (for salmon or any mild-flavored fish)

4 tablespoons butter
1 tablespoon minced onion
2½ tablespoons flour
¾ cup fish stock (see this page) or basic poaching liquid (see page 7)
1 teaspoon curry powder (more if desired)
¼ cup light cream

Melt butter in a small saucepan. Add onion and sauté until golden brown. Stir in flour and cook until bubbly. Gradually blend in the fish stock. Add curry powder and cream; stir until of desirable consistency. Makes about 8 servings.

Egg Sauce (for any fish)

3 tablespoons butter
3 tablespoons flour
1 cup fish stock (see this page) or basic poaching liquid (see page 7)
2 egg yolks, well-beaten

Melt butter over low heat; blend in the flour and cook until bubbly. Gradually stir in the hot fish stock; stir until the mixture begins to thicken. Remove from the heat and slowly stir the hot mixture into the egg yolks. Pour back into the pan and heat about 30 seconds. Serve hot over the fish. Makes enough for about 6 servings.

TOMATO SAUCE

The word *Portugaise* is often used to designate a tomato sauce. This one employs a short cut — canned stewed tomatoes. Its robust flavor is best suited to fish that have assertive flavors themselves.

Portugaise Sauce (for mackerel, rockfish, swordfish, albacore)

Sauté 1 medium-sized onion (chopped) in ¼ cup butter or margarine until soft. Add 1 crushed clove garlic, ½ teaspoon thyme, ¼ teaspoon crushed rosemary, and 1 can (1 lb.) stewed tomatoes (break up tomatoes with spoon). Simmer, uncovered, stirring occasionally, until reduced to about half; this takes about 15 minutes. Add salt and pepper to taste.

MAYONNAISE SAUCES

Mayonnaise is the base of a number of cold fish sauces. Use them on sizzling hot sautéed, broiled, or barbecued fish or on chilled poached fish. Here is an easy way to make mayonnaise sauces with a wire whip and round-bottomed bowl or your electric mixer. (If you happen to add oil too fast, causing the mayonnaise to separate, start again with 1 egg yolk in a clean bowl and slowly beat in the curdled mixture.)

Herb Mayonnaise Sauce (for any fish)

Put into the bowl 2 egg yolks, ½ teaspoon dry mustard, ½ teaspoon salt, ½ teaspoon thyme, ½ teaspoon tarragon, dash cayenne, 2 tablespoons chopped parsley, 1 tablespoon chopped chives, and 2 tablespoons lemon juice; beat until blended. Measure 1 cup salad oil (may be all or part olive oil); slowly add the oil (about 1 tablespoon at a time), beating constantly. As the mixture begins to get thick, you can beat in the oil more rapidly — in a slow stream. Beat in about 1 tablespoon hot water to make a good sauce consistency. Makes about 1½ cups.

Brown Butter Almond Sauce (for any fish, but best with salmon, halibut, trout)

Heat 1 cup (½ lb.) butter until it melts and turns a golden brown; cool to lukewarm. Following recipe for herb mayonnaise above, add mustard and cayenne to egg yolks, but omit the salt, herbs, parsley, and chives; reduce lemon to 1 tablespoon. Instead of salad oil, beat the browned butter into egg mixture exactly as directed for the mayonnaise above. Beat in 1 tablespoon dry sherry with the hot water. Then stir in ½ cup toasted, slivered almonds. If this becomes too stiff, beat in a little more hot water.

Rémoulade Sauce (for sole, rockfish, sea bass, halibut, trout)

Prepare the herb mayonnaise above, omitting salt, thyme, and chives; add 1 teaspoon anchovy paste and ½ teaspoon chervil to the egg mixture. After all oil has been added (omit water), stir in ¼ cup finely chopped dill pickle, 1 tablespoon chopped capers, and 2 hard-cooked eggs, chopped.

SIMPLE FISH SAUCES

Some fish sauces are simply made by stirring together mayonnaise, commercial sour cream, salad oil, or softened cream cheese with ingredients that give them their distinctive flavors. These are served on hot or chilled fish.

Tartare Sauce (for any fish)

½ cup mayonnaise (or ¼ cup mayonnaise and ¼ cup commercial sour cream)
¼ cup sweet pickle relish, well drained
1 teaspoon instant minced onion
¼ teaspoon Worcestershire
4 drops liquid hot-pepper seasoning
½ teaspoon lemon juice (or more to taste)

Combine all the ingredients. Cover and refrigerate at least 30 minutes or until needed. Makes about ¾ cup.

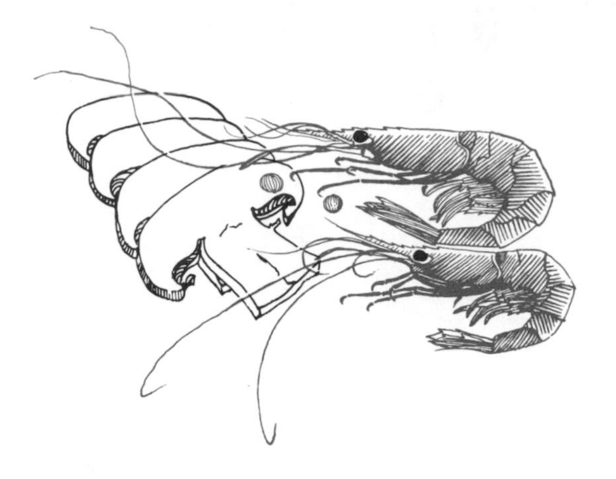

Cucumber Sauce (for any mild, white fish or salmon)

1 large package (8 oz.) cream cheese
2 egg yolks
2 tablespoons lemon juice
1 teaspoon seasoned salt
1/16 teaspoon pepper
1 tablespoon finely chopped green onion
1 cup coarsely grated or finely diced, peeled cucumber

Soften cream cheese; thoroughly blend in egg yolks, lemon juice, seasoned salt, pepper, and onion. Cook over low heat, stirring constantly, until thoroughly heated. Add cucumber (with excess moisture pressed out) and heat a few seconds longer. Serve warm. Makes about 1¾ cups sauce.

Sauce Gribiche (for any cold fish or shellfish)

Hard-cook 3 eggs; remove yolks and press them through a wire strainer. Mix with ½ teaspoon salt, 1 teaspoon dry mustard, ¼ teaspoon black pepper, ½ cup white wine vinegar, ¾ cup olive oil, ¾ cup salad oil, ½ cup chopped sour pickles, 2 teaspoons minced parsley, 2 teaspoons minced tarragon, 2 teaspoons minced chives, and the egg whites, finely chopped.

FREEZING FISH

Any fish or shellfish that is freshly caught may be frozen. The fish and shellfish you buy in the market may also be frozen if they have not been frozen before.

There has been a growing tendency in recent years to freeze certain fish and shellfish almost immediately after they are caught; sometimes freezing facilities are on the fishing boats. This is true of almost all shrimp, Alaska king crab, and abalone that are purchased. Much of the year (except during their summer seasons), the Pacific (Northern) halibut and swordfish in our markets have been frozen, even though they are defrosted in markets when you buy them. These will suffer in flavor and texture if they are refrozen, so be sure to inquire about any fish or shellfish you buy if you intend to freeze it.

To prepare fish for the freezer, eviscerate at once after catching. Pack in ice or grass to keep cool. Scale and dress as soon as possible. Cut in steaks, fillets, or baking-sized pieces. The head and tail may be left on small fish, if desired.

Place two pieces of waxed paper between steaks or fillets and wrap 2 to 4 pieces together in heavy freezer wrap. Seal completely. For larger pieces of fish, freeze, then dip in ice water. Refreeze, repeating the dipping and freezing until a thin, solid layer of ice has formed. Then wrap well in freezer wrap. Fish fillets, steaks, or small whole fish can be packed in rigid containers (milk cartons are good); cover with water and freeze; cover the top with freezer wrap. All the fat fish, such as salmon, hold best in flavor if frozen in ice this way.

For best flavor, salmon and other fat fish should be used within about 2 months. Lean fish keep well for a longer time.

Frozen fish is best defrosted in the refrigerator, for it loses juices more readily when thawed at room temperature. When you need to hasten thawing, immerse the wrapped package of fish briefly in cold, running water. Once thawed, fish should be used immediately. If fish is frozen in ice, allow to drain as it thaws, or immerse in cold running water to remove the ice coating; then thaw the fish in the refrigerator.

BUYING GUIDE FOR PACIFIC COAST FISH

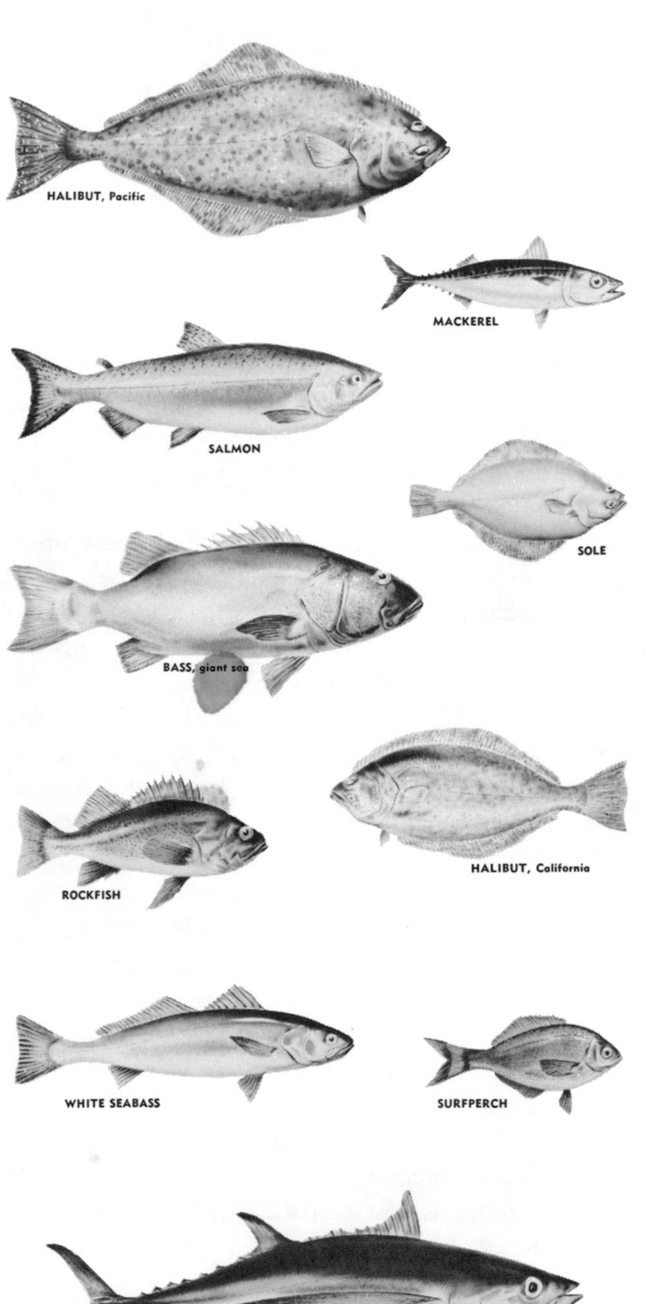

The fishes (and alternate names)	Flavor and texture?	How fat?
ALBACORE, Pacific (longfin tuna)	Rich flavor; soft flesh becomes firm and meaty when cooked	Moderate (over 5% fat)
BARRACUDA, California	Pronounced flavor; texture similar to dark meat tuna	Low (2 to 5% fat)
BASS, giant sea (black sea bass, grouper bass, seabass)	Mild flavor; tender white meat	Very low (under 2% fat)
COD, Pacific (true cod, gray cod, sea bass)	Mild flavor; very soft, white meat breaks apart easily when cooked	Very low
HALIBUT, California (flounder, halibut)	Mild flavor; tender white meat	Very low
HALIBUT, Pacific (northern halibut, 6 to 10-lb. size called chicken halibut)	Mild flavor; tender white meat	Very low
LINGCOD; not a cod (cultus cod)	Delicate flavor; white, tender flesh	Very low
MACKEREL, Pacific (blue, American)	Rich, pronounced flavor; dark meat, firm texture	Moderate
ROCKFISH (rock cod, sea bass, rosefish, grouper, red snapper, Pacific ocean perch, etc.)	Mild flavor; white to pink flesh becomes white and flaky when cooked	Very low
SABLEFISH (black cod, butterfish)	Buttery, mild flavor; fine, white, tender flesh	Moderate
SALMON; two main varieties: king (chinook, spring); silver (coho, silverside)	Rich, distinctive flavor; flesh is firm, white to bright red	Moderate
SHAD	Mild, meatlike flavor; quite bony, firm flesh	Moderate
SMELT, silversides (topsmelt, jacksmelt, grunion)	Mild, sweet flavor; fine tender flesh	Low
SMELT; true; includes salt and fresh water species (surf smelt, silver smelt, whitebait, Columbia river smelt)	Rich flavor that resembles trout; fine, firm flesh	Low to moderate
SOLE (petrale, rex, sand sole, sanddab, flounder, turbot)	Delicate flavor; fine grain, tender meat	Very low
STURGEON	Rich flavor; compact, meatlike flesh	Low
SURFPERCH; not true perch (sea perch; blue, white, silver sea perch)	Mild flavor; firm meat	Very low
SWORDFISH	Rich, distinctive flavor; firm, meatlike flesh	Low
WHITE SEABASS; also totuava, in same fish family	Mild flavor; white, tender flesh	Very low

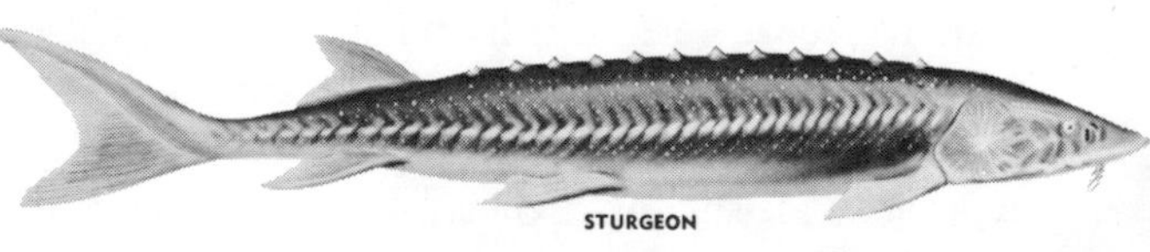

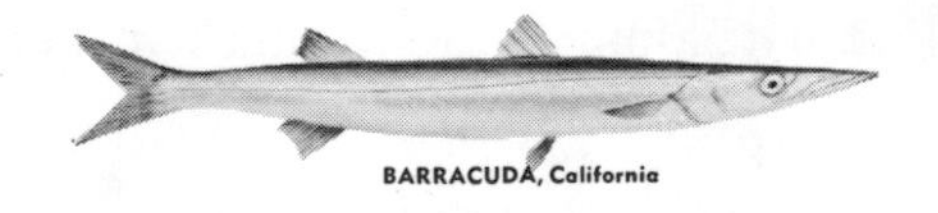

How big?	Forms available?	How to cook?	When available?	Where caught?	Where available?
10 to 25 lbs.	Whole (sometimes steaks, chunks)	Barbecue, broil, oven-fry steaks; poach or bake boneless chunks	Summer (midsummer through Oct. in Northwest)	Entire Pacific Coast	Entire Pacific Coast (on request at most markets)
4 to 7 lbs.	Whole, steaks, chunks	Barbecue, broil, bake in casseroles with well seasoned sauces	All year (most in spring and summer)	Southern Calif. and Mexico	Southern Calif. (limited amounts in Northern Calif.)
Up to 500 lbs.	Boneless chunks (fillets), sometimes whole steaks	Poach or bake large chunks or steaks; broil or fry thinner slices	All year	Southern Calif. and Mexico	Southern Calif.
3 to 20 lbs.	Fillets (occasionally whole in Northwest)	Poach or broil; cook in soups, stews, creamed dishes	All year	Northwest to Alaska	Northwest (frozen fillets in all markets)
4 to 25 lbs.	Whole, fillets, steaks	Broil, fry, butter-sauté, poach steaks and fillets; bake or poach whole fish	All year	Central Calif. into Mexico	Central and Southern Pacific Coast
6 to 75 lbs.	Steaks, fillets (small whole fish sometimes in Northwest)	Bake, broil, poach, oven-fry, or barbecue thick steaks, fillets; bake, poach small whole fish	May to Sept. (available frozen all year)	Northwest to Alaska	Northwest (some fresh fish in Calif.); frozen in all markets
5 to 20 lbs.	Whole, fillets, steaks	Broil, butter-sauté, fry, or poach fillets and steaks; bake or poach whole fish	All year (best April to Oct. in Calif.; Oct. to May in Northwest)	Entire Pacific Coast	Entire Pacific Coast
1 to 2 lbs.	Whole, fillets	Barbecue, broil, or bake with flavorful sauces	All year (peak is Sept. through Dec.)	Central and Southern Calif. and Mexico	Central and Southern Calif.
2 to 5 lbs.	Whole, fillets	Butter-sauté, broil, fry, poach, bake, or barbecue	All year	Entire Pacific Coast	Entire Pacific Coast
4 to 20 lbs.	Whole, fillets, steaks	Broil, barbecue, oven-fry, or bake	All year (best in summer in Calif.; Aug. to Nov. in Northwest)	Entire Pacific Coast	Entire Pacific Coast
6 to 30 lbs.	Whole, fillets, steaks	Barbecue, broil, bake, poach, or oven-fry	Varies by areas (frozen available all year)	Northern and Central Pacific Coast	Entire Pacific Coast
1½ to 7 lbs.	Whole	Bake or poach	March through May	Columbia River area	Northwest
2 to 12 fish per lb.	Whole	Butter-sauté, fry, or oven-fry	All year	Central and Southern Pacific Coast	Central and Southern Pacific Coast
8 to 12 fish per lb.	Whole (sometimes boneless whole fish in Northwest)	Butter-sauté, fry, or oven-fry	All year (most in spring and summer; Northwest river smelt Jan. to April)	Entire Pacific Coast	Entire Pacific Coast
¾ to 7 lbs.	Whole, fillets	Butter-sauté, broil, poach, oven-fry	All year	Entire Pacific Coast	Entire Pacific Coast
15 to 300 lbs.	Steaks, boneless chunks	Barbecue, broil, oven-fry, bake	All year (best March to Sept.)	Northern Pacific Coast	Northwest
½ to 3 lbs.	Whole	Butter-sauté, fry, oven-fry, broil	All year, except summer	Northern and Central Pacific Coast	Northwest and Central Pacific Coast
200 to 600 lbs.	Steaks, boneless chunks	Barbecue, broil, bake, oven-fry	Best Aug. through Oct. (available frozen all year)	Southern Calif. and Mexico	Southern Pacific Coast (frozen in all areas)
12 to 20 lbs. (totuava, 50 to 60 lbs.)	Steaks, fillets (small whole fish sometimes in Southwest); totuava steaks only	Broil, poach, oven-fry, or fry steaks or fillets; bake or poach whole seabass	Seabass all year (best in summer, fall); totuava in winter only	Southern Calif. and Mexico	Southern and Central Calif. (totuava Southern Calif. only)

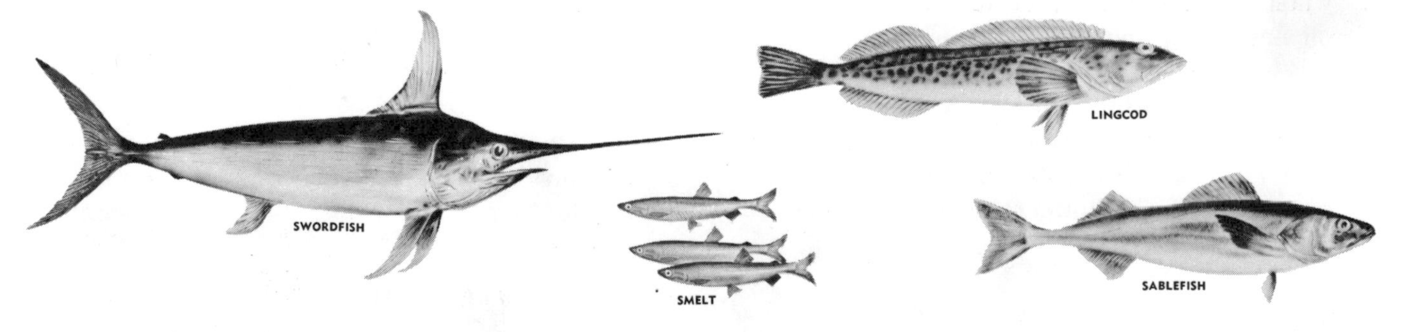

SOLE

Versatile Boneless Fillets

Some of the most delicately flavored and versatile fish available are sole. These small, flat fish are usually skinned and cut into fillets before they are sold fresh or in frozen packages. The resulting pieces of lean, white, boneless fish are thin and flexible; they may be cooked very quickly, or rolled or folded for a variety of elegant fish dishes.

The fish called sole in our markets are actually small members of the flounder family. The larger California halibut and much larger Pacific halibut are in the same family of fish. Any of these fish can easily be identified if seen whole, for all have flat bodies with both eyes on the same side of the head; the eye side of the body is colored, the blind side is white or gray.

Sole are all mild in flavor, with lean, white flesh, but varieties vary considerably in delicacy of flavor and fineness of texture. Connoisseurs usually rank the petrale as the most delicate, closely followed by the sanddab, sand sole, and rex sole. Other sole that you will see are English sole, Dover sole, starry flounder, and turbot. Sanddabs and rex sole are the smallest of these fish and are usually sold whole; all the others are usually sold as fillets.

The big advantage of buying sole at a fresh fish market is that you can choose the variety and size of fillets. Some of the recipes in this chapter specify approximate size or thickness of fillets to use. You may wish to buy sanddabs or other small sole whole and have the fish dealer clean the fish, trim off fins, head, and tail, and skin them. Prepared this way, sole may be cooked in some of the same ways as trout or other small whole fish.

For a quick meal or for breakfast, nothing could be finer than fresh sole, sautéed in butter and served with lemon-butter sauce (see page 5).

Grilled Sole

Here's a quick way to cook sole; it can be prepared right at the table on a sandwich grill.

Use small whole sole, dressed and skinned, or sole fillets. Dip each piece in melted butter and place on grill; close grids and cook at high temperature 2 to 4 minutes. (Have cup under drain spout to catch drippings.) Salt and pepper to taste and serve with parsley-flavored or onion-flavored butter; pass lemon wedges, if you wish.

Sole in Mushroom Sauce

An electric frying pan is most convenient for cooking this easy dish.

1 package (amount for 3 to 4 servings) dehydrated mushroom soup mix
½ pint (1 cup) sour cream
About ¼ teaspoon fines herbes or dash each *thyme, oregano, sweet basil, and marjoram*
3 tablespoons white wine, sherry, or milk
1 tablespoon lemon juice
2 tablespoons butter or margarine
1 pound sole fillets
Salt and pepper to taste
Chopped parsley or chives (optional)

In a small bowl, combine the soup mix, sour cream, fines herbes, white wine (or sherry or milk), and lemon juice. Meanwhile, melt the butter in your electric frying pan; have heat set at 225° (or set a frying pan over low heat). Lay fish fillets in melted butter and pour sour cream mixture over fish. Cover, reduce heat, and simmer gently for 7 minutes, or until fish flakes easily. Taste the sauce and add salt and pepper if needed. Remove fillets with sauce to a warm serving plate; sprinkle with chopped parsley or chives. Makes 3 to 4 servings.

Fillet of Sole Astoria

Well suited for a guest menu, rolled sole fillets are poached in the oven, then topped with a rich shrimp sauce. Serve them hot with buttered small red potatoes.

½ pound salmon, boned and skinned
1 tablespoon half-and-half (half cream, half milk)
¼ teaspoon salt
Dash pepper
12 small sole fillets
¼ cup frozen peas, thawed
1 teaspoon thinly sliced shallots or green onion
1 cup dry white wine
1 cup hot water
1½ tablespoons butter
1½ tablespoons flour
1 tablespoon lemon juice
About 1 cup cooked or canned small shrimp
Sliced shallots or green onion

Make a forcemeat with the salmon by chopping it fine, or grinding it. Mix in the half-and-half, salt, and pepper. Spread about 1½ tablespoons of the mixture over each of the sole fillets, covering only about three-fourths of each fillet. Sprinkle peas over the top of each fillet and gently roll each one toward the end which does not have filling on it. Secure the rolls by sticking a toothpick straight into each; then place them side by side in a baking dish or pan and spread shallots over the top. Add the wine and hot water and cover with foil; placc in a moderate oven (350°) and poach for 20 to 30 minutes, or until the meat will flake when probed with a fork. Remove fish rolls from the baking dish. Place on a serving platter and keep warm.

In a small pan, reduce the fish stock by half and stir in a roux made by blending until smooth the 1½ tablespoons butter and 1½ tablespoons flour. Cook, stirring constantly, until thickened. Pour sauce through a wire strainer (if you wish); add lemon juice and correct seasoning, if needed. Stir in the shrimp. Arrange fish rolls on a serving plate (with the cooked and seasoned potatoes, if you include them). Ladle the sauce over each fish roll. Garnish with shallot or green onion slices. Makes 6 servings.

Filbert-Crusted Sole

The distinctive flavor of filberts (hazelnuts) enhances this exquisite sole entrée.

4 large fillets of sole (about ½ pound each)
Salt and pepper
About ½ cup commercial sour cream
½ cup finely minced filberts
3 or 4 tablespoons butter or margarine
Lemon slices
Watercress

Sprinkle the sole fillets with salt and pepper. Spread each fillet on both sides with sour cream, and then coat each side in the minced filberts, spread on waxed paper. Heat the butter or margarine in a large frying pan (or chafing dish) until bubbling. Sauté sole fillets on each side until golden, turning only once. (Do not crowd fillets.) Serve from a heated platter, with butter from pan poured over fish. Garnish with lemon slices and watercress. Makes 4 servings.

Kauai Fillet of Sole

You can prepare Kauai fillet of sole (named for the Hawaiian isle) at the table in an electric frying pan; have ready the floured fillets, sliced avocado, and chopped macadamias. Small oriental teacups are ideal containers for the lime juice, extra butter, cream, and nuts.

4 large sole fillets (about 1 pound)
Salt and pepper
2 tablespoons lime juice
Flour
3 or 4 tablespoons butter or margarine
¼ cup heavy cream
1 large avocado, peeled, seeded, sliced lengthwise
¼ cup coarsely chopped macadamia nuts
Lime wedges

Sprinkle sole with salt and pepper and 1 tablespoon of the lime juice; let stand for 10 minutes. Dip fish in flour to coat all sides, shaking off the excess. At the table, heat about half the butter in an electric frying pan set at 350°; add fillets and sauté for 1 to 3 minutes, or until browned on one side. Turn fillets; add remaining butter and cook until nicely browned. Remove fish to a warm serving platter and sprinkle with remaining lime juice. To the pan, add the cream and bring to a rapid boil, scraping browned particles free; spoon over fish. Top with avocado slices and macadamia nuts. Serve at once. Pass lime wedges. Makes 4 servings.

Pescado en Concha

Discovered in Baja California, serve fish baked in a shell as a savory, hot appetizer or as a main dish.

½ cup water
½ cup dry white table wine
½ teaspoon salt
1 bay leaf
1 pound sole fillets
3 tablespoons butter or margarine
3 tablespoons flour
¼ cup half-and-half (half milk, half cream)
1 cup (¼ lb.) shredded medium-sharp Cheddar cheese

In a shallow pan, combine water, wine, salt, and bay leaf. Bring to a gentle boil and add fish. Cover and cook 3 or 4 minutes or until fish flakes. Remove from heat and drain broth from fish, saving ¾ cup of it. Discard bay leaf. Break fish into small pieces. Melt butter in a saucepan and blend in flour. Gradually add the ¾ cup broth and the cream. Cook, stirring, until thickened. Add ½ cup of the cheese and blend until melted; add fish. Spoon this mixture into individual baking dishes (scallop shells if you have them) and sprinkle evenly with remaining cheese. Bake in a moderately hot oven (375°) until bubbling, about 10 minutes. (You can fill the shells ahead of time, refrigerate, and bake before serving.) Makes 3 to 4 entrée-sized servings, or 6 appetizer-sized servings.

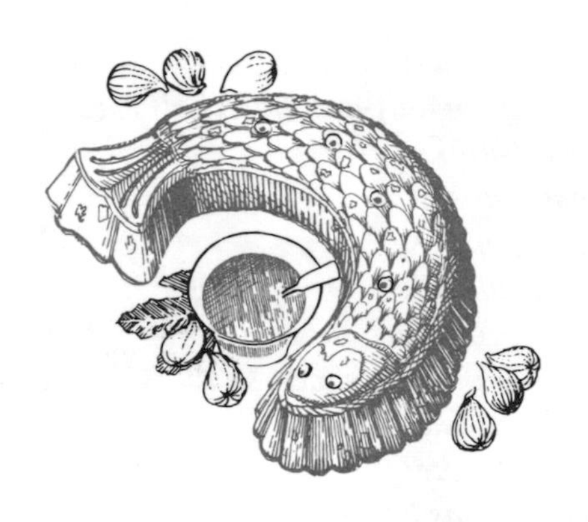

Mushroom-Baked Sole

A mushroom filling complements these wine-baked sole fillets.

1 medium-sized onion, finely chopped
¼ cup chopped parsley
1 cup sliced mushrooms (about 4 large)
¼ cup (⅛ lb.) butter or margarine
8 sole fillets (about 1½ lbs.)
Salt and pepper
¼ cup dry white wine
½ cup half-and-half (half milk, half cream)
1 tablespoon flour
Paprika
Chopped parsley

Sauté onion, parsley, and mushrooms in 3 tablespoons of the butter for about 10 minutes, until onions are soft, stirring occasionally. Place 4 of the sole fillets, flat, in a greased baking dish (about 9 by 13 inches); sprinkle lightly with salt and pepper. Spread sautéed mixture evenly over sole; top with remaining 4 fillets and sprinkle with salt and pepper. Pour on wine; dot with remaining 1 tablespoon butter. Bake, uncovered, in a moderate oven (350°) for 15 minutes. Remove from oven. Drain off pan liquid; reserve.

Gradually stir half-and-half into flour in a small pan; blend in fish liquid. Cook, stirring constantly, until thickened. Pour over fish. Bake for 5 minutes longer, until fish flakes easily with a fork. Sprinkle with paprika and parsley. Makes 4 servings.

Sole with Shallots in Cream

Here you poach shallots and mushrooms with sole fillets. You will achieve a different, less subtle flavor if you substitute green onions for the shallots.

¼ cup finely chopped shallots or green onions
2 teaspoons finely chopped parsley
¼ pound mushrooms, sliced
1 pound sole fillets
½ cup dry white wine
Salt and pepper
1 cup (½ pt.) heavy cream
Parsley sprigs
Cherry tomatoes

Arrange shallots, parsley, and mushrooms over the bottom of a wide frying pan. Lay sole fillets on top of this mixture, overlapping as little as possible. Pour wine over the fish (the liquid will not cover the fillets). Cover the pan and bring liquid quickly to a boil. Reduce heat and simmer gently for about 3 to 5 minutes, or until fish turns opaque and flakes easily. With a wide spatula, carefully transfer just the fillets to a hot serving dish, and keep warm. Salt and pepper to taste.

Add cream to the frying pan and boil rapidly until sauce is reduced to about the consistency of medium white sauce and takes on a pale golden color. Watch carefully; sauce scorches if reduced too much. Season with salt and pepper to taste. Pour evenly over the fillets; garnish with parsley sprigs and cherry tomtaoes. Makes 4 servings.

Fillet of Sole Bonne Femme

White wine, cream, and mushrooms are the ingredients in *bonne femme* sauce. A version of this sauce is served here over baked sole fillets.

8 medium-sized sole fillets (about 1½ lbs.)
Salt and white pepper
2 green onions, sliced, including part of tops
2 whole lemons, thinly sliced
½ cup dry white wine
Water
½ pound mushrooms, sliced
¼ cup butter or margarine
2 tablespoons flour
2 egg yolks
2 tablespoons heavy cream
Chopped parsley
Lemon wedges

Sprinkle sole lightly with salt and pepper. Fold fillets crosswise and place in a greased baking pan, about 10 inches square or round. Top with onions and lemon slices; pour on wine. Cover and bake in a hot oven (400°) for 15 to 20 minutes, or until fish flakes easily when tested with a fork. Remove from oven; discard lemon slices. Drain pan liquid into a measuring cup; add water to make 1 cup. Keep sole warm in pan. Sauté mushroom slices in butter until lightly browned. Stir in flour until bubbly. Gradually add liquid mixture and cook, stirring constantly, until thickened. Beat egg yolks with cream; stir in a little of the hot liquid. Return egg mixture to pan and cook, stirring constantly, until thickened.

Lift sole onto a warm, deep serving platter. Blend about 1 tablespoon of the additional pan liquid into the mushroom sauce to thin it slightly, if you wish. Spoon mushroom sauce evenly over the sole, and serve immediately. Garnish with lemon wedges and parsley. Makes 4 to 6 servings.

Sole à la Wickett

Poached sole fillets are arranged on a plank or oven-proof platter, then bordered with mashed potatoes (put through a pastry bag) for a fine company dish. You can do most preparation ahead.

8 fillets of sole (about ⅓ lb. each*)*
Salt and pepper
2 tablespoons butter
2 medium-sized onions
1 clove garlic
10 whole black peppers
1 bay leaf
¾ cup dry white wine
¼ cup water
3 tablespoons butter or margarine
3 tablespoons flour
¼ teaspoon salt
Dash of cayenne
½ cup plus 2 tablespoons half-and-half (half milk, half cream)
2 packages (amount for 4 servings each*) instant mashed potatoes*
8 large whole mushroom crowns, sautéed in butter
2 teaspoons crushed chervil

Sprinkle each piece of fish on one side with salt and pepper; dot each with about ¾ teaspoon of the 2 tablespoons butter. Fold each piece over in half lengthwise and place in a shallow baking dish. Cut the onions and garlic in thin slices; scatter over sole. Sprinkle with peppers; tuck in bay leaf. Add the wine and water. Cover and poach in a moderate oven (350°) for 15 minutes. Drain and save the fish stock; discard onions, garlic, pepper, and bay. (If you plan to serve the dish right away, keep fish warm; otherwise, refrigerate it.) Handle folded pieces carefully, for they fall apart easily.

Melt the 3 tablespoons butter in a pan; blend in the flour, ¼ teaspoon salt, and cayenne. Slowly stir in the reserved fish stock and the half-and-half; stirring constantly, cook until thickened. (You can use the sauce immediately or reheat.) Arrange the fish on a board or ovenproof platter. Prepare the mashed potatoes according to package directions; put through a pastry bag using rosette tip, and make a solid decorative edge around the board. Spoon hot sauce over fish and garnish with the sautéed mushrooms; sprinkle with the chervil. Place in a very hot oven (450°) for about 5 to 7 minutes to lightly brown the potato border. Makes 6 to 8 servings.

Sole and Crab Mousse

Sole and crab mousse makes a decorative supper entrée when baked in individual fish molds. The shrimp sauce topping is served separately.

¾ pound sole fillets or ¾ pound boneless white, lean fish fillet
¼ pound crab meat
2 egg yolks
2 eggs, separated
¾ cup half-and-half (half milk, half cream)
3 tablespoons flour
1 teaspoon salt
⅛ teaspoon nutmeg
1 tablespoon lemon juice
1 tablespoon brandy
½ pint (1 cup) whipping cream
Shrimp sauce (recipe follows)

Purée in a blender the sole fillets and crab meat and turn into a bowl. Add the 4 egg yolks, one at a time, and beat until smooth. Beat in the half-and-half, flour, salt, nutmeg, lemon juice, and brandy. Whip cream until stiff and fold in. Beat egg whites until stiff, but not dry, and fold in. Turn into 6 buttered individual baking molds or fish molds. Place in a pan of hot water and bake in a moderate oven (350°) for 25 minutes, or until puffed and set. Let cool 10 minutes; then invert on a serving plate. Serve with shrimp sauce (recipe follows). Makes 6 servings.

SHRIMP SAUCE:

Reduce 2 cups fish stock (see directions for fish stock on page 9 in the first chapter) to 1 cup by boiling. Beat 2 egg yolks until light and blend in 2 teaspoons cornstarch and ½ cup light cream; pour in the hot fish stock, stirring until blended. Cook over low heat, stirring constantly until thickened. Stir in 1 tablespoon dry sherry and ½ cup cooked shrimp, crab, or lobster meat. Heat.

Light and airy sole and crab mousse makes a decorative supper entrée when baked in individual fish molds. Spoon shrimp sauce over the mousse and serve it with fresh asparagus spears.

Oyster-Stuffed Sole Florentine

You arrange these poached fish with buttery, nutmeg-seasoned spinach. The creamy sauce spooned over all is especially easy to make.

8 large oysters
8 thin fillets of sole (about 1¾ lbs.)
1 bottle (8 oz.) clam juice
3 cups hot cooked chopped spinach
2 tablespoons butter
½ teaspoon nutmeg
Salt and pepper to taste
1 can (10½ oz.) cream of celery soup
2 teaspoons Worcestershire
2 tablespoons chopped green onion
2 tablespoons grated Parmesan cheese

Roll an oyster in each piece of sole; fasten with toothpicks. In a frying pan, bring clam juice to a boil. Carefully slip in sole; cover and simmer for 3 or 4 minutes. Remove the toothpicks from sole and save the stock.

Season well drained spinach with butter, nutmeg, salt, and pepper; arrange in a baking dish in alternate rows with sole (or cover bottom of dish with spinach and arrange sole on top).

Boil fish stock rapidly until reduced about one half. Blend in celery soup, Worcestershire, and green onion. Bring to a boil and spoon over fish and spinach. Sprinkle with cheese and place in a hot oven (400°) for 5 to 7 minutes, or until all ingredients are piping hot. (Another good way to arrange this entrée is to mound spinach in the center of the baking dish and surround with the oyster-stuffed sole.) Makes 4 to 6 servings.

LEAN, MILD FISH

Halibut, Rockfish, Lingcod, Pacific Cod, Seabass

When cooking fish, you will encounter recipes which specify only lean, white fish fillets. In such recipes, you can usually use sole (see chapter on Sole) or any of the fish described in this chapter—halibut, rockfish, lingcod, seabass, and cod. In the pages that follow, you will find recipes using these fish interchangeably.

Although all of the fish described here generally classify as lean, white, and mild-flavored, they often differ immensely in size, shape, and bone structure. Each type of fish is discussed individually to enable you to understand its special characteristics and thereby to discover many more ways to cook it.

CALIFORNIA HALIBUT AND PACIFIC HALIBUT

Two types of halibut are found in our markets; both are members of the flounder family and thus are flat with both eyes on the same side of the head. The difference lies mainly in size. California halibut ranges from about 4 to 25 pounds; Pacific halibut, often called northern halibut, is a larger fish, weighing up to about 75 pounds. Both are very fine tasting fish, but Pacific halibut is considered more choice.

Landed in central and southern California ports, California halibut can be purchased at the fresh fish markets in these areas most of the year. Much of this halibut is sold as boneless fillets, but you will sometimes find small whole fish in markets.

Pacific halibut is landed in the Northwest. A large proportion of the catch is cut into thick steaks or fillets and shipped frozen all over the country. In summer, during the height of the Pacific halibut season in the Northwest, you can sometimes buy a small 6 to 10-pounder, called a chicken halibut. This is an especially good buy; it is of lower value commercially because chicken halibut is too small a fish to make good steaks.

A small halibut (either California or Pacific) is a good choice when you wish to bake and serve a whole fish (see recipes pages 22 and 24). Another alternative is to have these small fish cut into two whole fillets (with skin on) for barbecuing; you can prepare the fillets the same as for barbecued sablefish on page 41, increasing the amount of butter in the baste to 1 cup.

The usual size and thickness of halibut steaks and fillets make them well suited for broiling, poaching, frying, or oven-frying; thin pieces of halibut may even be butter-sautéed (see basic cooking methods in the first chapter).

ROCKFISH

Fifty or more varieties of rockfish may be found on the Pacific coast. All are similar in shape (a large head in proportion to body), but they vary widely in color. The orange and red varieties are sometimes sold whole in fresh fish markets; the more drab colored ones are usually sold as fillets.

For some reason, fish markets almost never display these fish by the name of rockfish; most often you will find them called rock cod. You will see red rockfish often labeled red snapper, snapper, or rosefish. A particularly good tasting black rockfish in the Northwest is sold under the name of black sea bass or sea bass. And packaged frozen fillets of rockfish are frequently labeled Pacific ocean perch.

When you find whole fresh rockfish, they weigh about 2 to 5 pounds and lend themselves to some interesting recipes (several are included in this chapter). The skinned rockfish fillets, which are quite mild in flavor, may be butter-sautéed, broiled, poached, fried, or oven-fried; these basic cooking methods are discussed in the first chapter.

LINGCOD

These lean, mild fish are plentiful all up and down the Pacific coast. They have a neat, rounded shape, similar to that of salmon, and range in size from 5 to 20 pounds.

Whole lingcod may be stuffed and baked (see page 24). It may also be cut crosswise into neat, serving-sized steaks, or cut lengthwise on either side of the bone to make thick fillets for barbecuing or broiling (see page 25). Lingcod steaks and fillets are suitable for poaching, frying, and broiling (follow directions for lean fish). Thinner pieces may be butter-sautéed. These basic cooking methods are described in the first chapter.

PACIFIC COD

Because Pacific cod are caught exclusively in northern Pacific waters, you will find them fresh only in markets of the Northwest. But frozen packaged cod fillets can be found in all markets. The markets which handle fresh Pacific cod often label it as true cod to distinguish it from lingcod and other fish having the word "cod" in their names.

Like other lean, white fish, cod is mild in flavor, but has especially soft meat that flakes apart readily when cooked. This accounts for the fact that some of the most popular cod dishes have a creamy base (see page 26). The poached and flaked meat of cod is excellent for use in salads and casserole dishes. Cod also makes a good fish chowder. A good way to handle the fish fillets is to oven-fry them; oven-frying is discussed on page 7 in the first chapter. Cod fillets can also be used in many recipes that call for sole fillets, provided that rolling or handling the cooked fish is not required.

Salt-cured cod is prepared from Atlantic caught cod, a similar fish to Pacific cod. Salt cod is available in most markets, and several recipes for its use are given in this chapter.

GIANT SEA BASS AND WHITE SEABASS

Landed in Southern California ports, giant sea bass and white seabass are often confused because of the similarity of their names. A third very similar fish is the totuava, caught in the Gulf of California and imported from Mexico into Southern California markets.

The giant sea bass is a huge fish, weighing up to about 500 pounds. Until recently, its official name was black sea bass, so it is often still called by this name, as well as grouper bass.

The white seabass is actually a croaker, not a bass at all, and the totuava is in the same fish family. White seabass ranges in size from about 12 to 20 pounds and has a sleek body shape like that of salmon. Totuava is a larger fish, usually 45 to 60 pounds.

During summer and fall, when most of the white seabass are landed, Southern California markets sometimes have small, whole 12 to 15-pound fish; these are a nice size to bake whole (see page 27), or to have cut into two long fillets (skin left on) for barbecuing. To barbecue white seabass fillets, follow the directions for barbecued sablefish on page 41, increasing the amount of butter in the baste to 1 cup.

White seabass is commonly available as fillets or steaks. Totuava and giant sea bass are cut into large thick steaks. A thick, whole steak of giant sea bass makes a meal for about six people. The firm, white flesh of any of these fish is delicious poached or baked. Serving-sized portions may also be broiled, barbecued, fried, or oven-fried (see basic cooking methods given in first chapter). Some salmon recipes, given in the next chapter, are also suitable for these fish.

Halibut Baked in a Crust

You can bake California halibut or a small Pacific halibut in a crust. Have the skin peeled off the top of the fish (about 8 pounds, whole weight). Rub inside and outside with salt and pepper. Put into a baking pan lined with 5 slices bacon. With a spoon, make a smooth dough of 1 cup soft butter and 1 cup unsifted flour. Roll out on a lightly floured board to fit top of fish; arrange on fish. Cut 2 more slices bacon in small pieces and place on top of dough. Bake in a hot oven (400°) for about 30 minutes, until fish flakes easily. If necessary, slip under broiler for a few minutes to brown crust. Stir about 1 teaspoon lemon juice and 2 tablespoons cream into the drippings for a sauce to serve with the fish. Makes about 8 servings.

Halibut Curry

The unusual garnishes of Polynesian-flavored halibut curry make it an ideal dish for guest meals.

About 3 pounds halibut or other firm, lean, white fish fillets
½ cup (¼ lb.) butter
1½ teaspoons curry powder
8 bananas
½ cup chopped peanuts
¼ cup toasted, salted coconut chips
½ cup tiny pearl onions

Poach halibut fillets as directed on pages 6-7. Melt butter and stir in curry powder. Cut bananas lengthwise and sauté in curry butter. Remove bananas from pan and keep warm. Lightly brown chopped peanuts in the same pan. Arrange the halibut and bananas on a warm platter. Spoon the peanuts and melted butter over the fillets. Garnish with coconut chips and onions. Serve immediately. Makes 8 servings.

Barbecued Halibut

You can barbecue thick boneless pieces of any firm-fleshed, lean white fish using this method.

Cut a 4-pound fillet of halibut or other firm, white fish into pieces about 1 inch wide, 2 inches long, and 1 inch thick. Combine ½ cup soy sauce, 1 cup dry white wine, 2 tablespoons lemon juice, 2 cloves garlic (minced or mashed), 1 teaspoon powdered ginger, and ½ cup salad oil. Pour over fish pieces and marinate 4 hours. Pour off marinade and save. Sprinkle fish pieces generously with about 2 tablespoons fresh rosemary and about 6 tablespoons fresh chopped parsley. Skewer carefully or slip inside a hinged wire broiler and place on the grill over low coals. Cook until fish flakes when tested with a fork, about 10 to 15 minutes, basting occasionally with part of the marinade.

In the meantime, sauté 1 pound sliced fresh mushrooms in ⅓ cup butter; add remaining marinade, heat through, and pour over broiled fish. Makes 8 servings.

Glazed Fillet of Halibut or White Seabass

This baking method may be used for a whole fillet (skin left on) from California halibut, white seabass, or lingcod, or for boneless portions and steaks of giant sea bass or Pacific halibut. If you reduce the baking time to 10 to 15 minutes, the recipe can also be used for serving-sized steaks and fillets of these fish.

Put 1 whole fillet (from a 12-pound fish, whole weight), skin side down in a greased baking pan. Brush top with butter; sprinkle with salt and pepper. Bake in a hot oven (425°) for 25 to 30 minutes, or until the fish flakes easily. Meanwhile, combine 1 cup commercial sour cream with 1 teaspoon dry mustard, 1 teaspoon dill weed or chopped fresh dill, and ½ cup cooked or canned small shrimp (optional). Remove the fish from the oven; spread with the sour cream and heat under the broiler for about 3 minutes, or just until the top is glazed and browned. Makes 6 servings.

Baked Halibut with Dill Stuffing

A stuffing is baked between layers of fish fillets for this dish, with sliced onions and tomatoes on top.

3 pounds halibut or other lean, white fillets
1 cup soft bread crumbs
¼ cup melted butter
3 tablespoons chopped dill pickle
2 tablespoons finely chopped green pepper
2 tablespoons finely chopped onion
¼ teaspoon salt
¼ teaspoon white pepper
1 egg, beaten
1 medium-sized onion, very thinly sliced
1 tomato, thinly sliced
Salt, pepper, and sweet basil

Place half the fish in the bottom of a greased shallow baking dish. Mix together stuffing of bread crumbs, butter, dill pickle, green pepper, onion, salt, pepper, and egg. Spread stuffing over fish in baking dish. Cover with remaining fish. On top of fish, arrange onion slices, then tomato slices. Sprinkle with salt, pepper and sweet basil. Bake, uncovered, in a moderate oven (350°) for 45 minutes, or until fish flakes with a fork. Makes 6 to 8 servings.

Halibut with Wine and Lemon

Mild halibut or lingcod responds well to this method of cooking. The fish is first marinated in a lemon and wine mixture, then browned in butter. The marinade becomes the basis of the sauce served over the halibut.

6 halibut or lingcod steaks or fillets (about 2 lbs.)
1 egg
4 tablespoons lemon juice
1¼ cups dry white table wine
½ teaspoon salt
⅛ teaspoon pepper
4 tablespoons butter or margarine
1 tablespoon minced parsley

Arrange fish steaks in a single layer and close together in a shallow pan. Beat together egg, 3 tablespoons of the lemon juice, 1 cup of the wine, salt, and pepper, and pour over the fish. Cover lightly and chill for about 1 hour. Lift fish from marinade, draining. Heat 2 tablespoons of the butter in a wide frying pan; add fish steaks and brown on both sides. Place fish on a heated platter in a warm place. In pan, melt the remaining 2 tablespoons butter; add ¼ cup of the marinade, the remaining 1 tablespoon lemon juice, and ¼ cup wine. Bring to a rapid boil. Pour some of sauce over the fish and pass the remainder to add to each serving. Sprinkle with minced parsley. Makes 6 servings.

Basque-Style Halibut Steaks

Squeeze juice of 1 lemon over 4 large halibut steaks (totaling 1½ to 2 lbs.) and let stand a few minutes. Sprinkle steaks with salt and pepper. Beat 1 egg with a fork until frothy; dip the steaks and coat on all sides. Then dust fish with flour, shaking off the excess.

Heat 3 or 4 tablespoons olive oil in a wide frying pan with 2 whole cloves garlic and cook until garlic begins to brown. Place halibut in pan and cook over medium high heat until steaks are lightly browned on one side. Turn and cook until other side is browned and fish flakes easily; takes 8 to 10 minutes. Serve with lemon slices and garnish with parsley or watercress. Makes 4 servings.

Two Rockfish, Stuffed and Baked

When you shop at a fresh fish market, consider picking out two whole rockfish of about the same size; have the dealer dress them and cut out the back bones. The fish will then open out flat and be almost boneless; you can bake them, one on top of the other, with stuffing between.

1 small onion, chopped
1 cup sliced almonds
6 tablespoons butter
1 cup dry bread crumbs
¾ teaspoon salt
½ teaspoon rubbed sage
⅛ teaspoon pepper
2 rockfish (4 to 5 pounds each, whole weight), dressed and boned
2 tablespoons melted butter
2 tablespoons dry bread crumbs

Prepare the almond stuffing as follows: Sauté the onion and almonds in the 6 tablespoons butter for about 5 minutes. Add the 1 cup bread crumbs, salt, sage, and pepper. Spread between the rockfish, opened out flat and arranged in a greased baking pan one on top of the other; skin sides of fish should be on bottom and top. Brush the top with the 2 tablespoons melted butter and sprinkle with the 2 tablespoons bread crumbs. Bake, uncovered, in a moderately hot oven (375°) for about 35 minutes, or until fish flakes easily. Makes 6 to 8 servings.

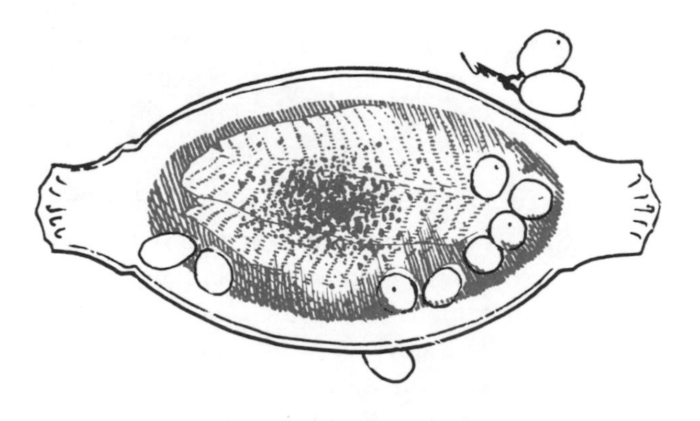

Rockfish in Foil

Have a whole rockfish dressed and it is ready to be wrapped in foil and baked or barbecued.

⅔ cup soy sauce
¼ cup olive oil or salad oil
1 large clove garlic, minced
1 teaspoon ground ginger
1 whole rockfish (3 to 5 pounds, whole weight), dressed

Prepare a teriyaki sauce by combining the soy sauce, olive oil or salad oil, garlic, and ginger. Pour over the whole prepared fish in a shallow pan; marinate for about 30 minutes, turning fish several times. Remove from marinade; wrap tightly in heavy foil and bake in a hot oven (425°) until the fish flakes, 30 to 40 minutes. If you prefer, barbecue the foil-wrapped fish for about the same length of time, turning several times. Makes 4 servings.

Stuffed Baked Lingcod or Halibut

Have ready a 6 to 8-pound lingcod or California halibut (whole weight), dressed and washed. (If you buy halibut, ask the dealer to remove the backbone to allow more room for the stuffing.) Prepare this stuffing: Melt ¼ cup (⅛ lb.) butter or margarine; sauté 1 cup sliced fresh mushrooms. Stir in 4 cups chopped fresh spinach (about 1 pound) or 2 packages (10 oz. *each*) frozen chopped spinach, thawed, with ¼ cup chopped sweet onion, 1½ teaspoons dill weed, ¼ cup fine dry bread crumbs, 1 teaspoon salt, and dash pepper. Stuff the fish cavity; close opening with skewers. Put into a greased baking pan; brush with mixture of 4 tablespoons melted butter and 4 tablespoons lemon juice. Bake, uncovered, in a moderately hot oven (375°) for about 45 minutes, or until fish flakes, basting several times with the lemon-butter. Serve with some of the pan drippings spooned over top. Makes 6 servings.

Curried Lingcod

Try this method of pan-frying fish for lingcod steaks or for serving-sized fillets of rockfish or halibut (about ¾ to 1 inch thick).

Combine 2 tablespoons minced onion, 1 clove garlic (minced or mashed), 1 teaspoon curry powder, ½ teaspoon salt, and a generous dash cayenne. Rub over both sides of 4 fish steaks or fillets (about 1½ to 2 pounds). Cover fish; allow to stand in the refrigerator for 3 hours. Dust fish with flour to coat both sides. Heat about 1½ tablespoons butter and 1½ tablespoons salad oil in a frying pan over moderately high heat; brown fish pieces on both sides. Serve with parsley, lemon wedges, and chutney. Makes 4 servings.

Grilled Lingcod

This easy-to-prepare dish can be cooked in the broiler or on the barbecue. Buy unskinned lingcod fillets (2 lbs. for 4 servings). Baste with melted butter; season with salt and pepper and place over a slow heat on your barbecue or, if broiling indoors, place 10 inches from heat. To barbecue, place skin side down; cook 10 minutes; then turn and cook 3 minutes more. To oven-broil cook 6 minutes on each side. (This is especially good prepared on a covered smoke barbecue; use same cooking times.)

Lingcod Florentine

A light golden sauce tops a layer of spinach and poached fish in lingcod Florentine. Rockfish or halibut fillets may also be cooked this way.

2½ pounds lingcod fillets
1 package (10 oz.) frozen spinach
1 tablespoon butter
1 cup medium white sauce
1 egg yolk, well beaten
½ cup grated Parmesan cheese
½ cup whipping cream
Parmesan cheese

Poach the fillets in poaching liquid as directed on pages 6-7. Cook frozen spinach as directed on the package; drain thoroughly. Arrange spinach in bottom of a buttered, shallow 2-quart baking dish and layer the fish fillets on top of the spinach. To make the sauce, melt butter and add it to the white sauce (your own recipe or canned). Slowly blend sauce with the egg yolk; fold in ½ cup grated Parmesan cheese and the cream. Pour sauce over the fish. Sprinkle additional Parmesan on top. Brown lightly under the broiler. Makes 6 servings.

Baked Fish Fillet

For this recipe buy a 2-pound whole fillet of lingcod, California halibut, or white seabass and have it cut into 2 pieces of about equal size; you can also use 2 rockfish fillets, each weighing about 1 pound.

2-pound fillet of lingcod, halibut, seabass, or rockfish
3 slices bacon, chopped
1 small onion, diced
½ cup light cream or undiluted evaporated milk
3 tablespoons lemon juice
1 small dill pickle, diced
½ teaspoon prepared mustard
1 tablespoon parsley
1 tablespoon cornstarch
2 tablespoons melted butter
½ cup shredded sharp Cheddar cheese
2 tablespoons fine dry bread crumbs

Arrange one piece of fish in a greased baking dish. Sauté the bacon until browned in a small frying pan; add onion to the pan and cook until golden. Remove from heat and cool slightly. Stir in the light cream or evaporated milk, lemon juice, pickle, mustard, parsley, and cornstarch; mix until the cornstarch is well blended. Pour over the fish. Set the second piece of fish over the filling. Brush the top with melted butter; sprinkle with cheese and bread crumbs. Bake, uncovered, in a moderately hot oven (375°) for about 25 minutes. Makes about 6 servings.

Fresh Pacific Cod in Cream Sauce

Remove skin from 3 pounds fresh Pacific cod or defrost frozen cod fillets; cut into about 1½-inch cubes. Melt 1 tablespoon butter in the bottom of a heavy kettle with a tight-fitting lid; put fish pieces into it. Add 8 whole allspice, 1½ teaspoons salt, and 1 teaspoon sugar; mix in gently. Gradually blend 2 cups water into 3 tablespoons flour to make a smooth paste; pour over fish. Cover and simmer gently until the fish is tender, about 15 minutes. With a slotted spoon, remove fish to serving dish. To the cooking stock, add juice of ½ lemon and 1 egg yolk, beaten with 3 tablespoons cream; cook, stirring for about 3 minutes; pour over fish. Makes 6 servings.

Codfish in Cream

Prepare salted codfish the night before to reheat for breakfast. Serve it also for a family supper.

1 package (1 lb.) salted codfish
Water
1 medium-sized onion, sliced
1 lemon, sliced
2 whole cloves
3 whole black peppers
¼ cup (⅛ lb.) butter
¼ cup flour
½ cup milk
1½ cups diced cooked potatoes
2 hard-cooked eggs, sliced
Finely chopped parsley
About 2 tablespoons canned crisp bacon rinds

Early the day before, cover salted codfish with cold water; allow to stand several hours. Pour off water; rinse fish.

Fill a kettle with enough water to cover fish. Bring water to a boil; add onion, lemon, cloves, and a few whole black peppers. Add fish, reduce heat to simmering; cook until fish is tender, about 20 to 30 minutes. Pour off liquid and strain; save 1 cup. In another saucepan, melt butter. Stir in flour to make a smooth paste. Gradually add milk and the 1 cup reserved liquid, stirring until smooth and thickened. Add codfish. (When preparing for the following morning, cool, then refrigerate overnight; next morning, reheat.)

Arrange potatoes on heated serving platter or 4 individual serving plates. Top with sliced eggs, and a little finely chopped parsley. Serve codfish over potatoes and eggs. Sprinkle with canned crisp bacon rinds. Makes 4 generous servings.

Salt-Cod, Basque Style

Bacalao is the name for salted cod in the Spanish Basque country. There are dozens of ways of preparing it, but this is one of the most typical.

1 pound salted codfish
2 cloves garlic
2 tablespoons olive oil or salad oil
2 tablespoons water
1 small onion, chopped (about ⅓ cup)
1 clove garlic, minced or mashed
3 tablespoons olive oil or salad oil
3 tablespoons finely chopped parsley
1 can (8 oz.) tomato sauce
1 cup broth or water
Dash pepper
Salt to taste
2 cups diced boiled potatoes
2 canned pimientos, chopped
3 tablespoons fine dry bread crumbs, mixed with 1 tablespoon butter

Freshen the cod by soaking it overnight in cold water. Or soak it for several hours, changing the water several times. Drain and cover with fresh cold water, bring to a boil, then discard water; repeat this process if the water tastes salty. Heat the 2 cloves garlic in the 2 tablespoons oil; add water and the drained cod fillets. Cover and simmer for 5 to 10 minutes. Drain and arrange the fish in a shallow baking dish (about 9 inches square). Cook the onion and mashed garlic in the 3 tablespoons oil until soft; add parsley and cook about 5 minutes. Add the tomato sauce, broth or water, pepper, and salt to taste; mix well. Add the potatoes and pimientos, and pour over the fish. Sprinkle with the buttered crumbs. Bake, uncovered, in a moderate oven (350°) for 25 to 30 minutes. Makes 4 to 6 servings.

Baked Whole White Seabass

Smaller white seabass are a good shape and size for baking whole. Place a dressed fish (about 12 pounds, whole weight) in a large baking pan or roasting pan. Sprinkle inside and outside of fish with salt and pepper. Pour over it a mixture of 1 cup dry white wine and 1 cup sliced green onions. Add 2 bay leaves to the pan and arrange thin slices of 1 whole lemon on top of the fish. Cover tightly with foil or the top of the roaster. Bake in a moderate oven (350°) for about 1 hour, or until the fish flakes. Sauté ½ pound sliced mushrooms in ¼ cup (⅛ lb.) butter for about 5 minutes. When the fish is cooked, drain off pan juices; blend juices with 2 teaspoons cornstarch, and stir into the pan of mushrooms; cook until thickened. Stir in about ½ cup canned or cooked small shrimp; heat mixture through and serve with fish. Makes 15 to 20 servings.

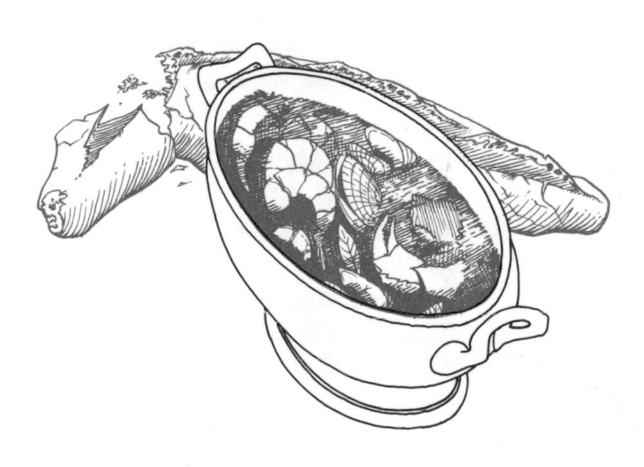

Poached Bass with Rémoulade

A whole giant seabass steak can be poached and served with rémoulade sauce; you can also use a large Pacific halibut steak.

In a pan large enough to hold the whole bass steak (about 2½ pounds), bring to a boil 1 quart of water with 4 teaspoons salt, 8 whole allspice, and half a medium-sized onion, sliced. Set in the fish; simmer until it flakes, about 6 to 8 mi[illegible] Carefully remove fish to a hot plate; sprinkle chopped parsley and serve with a sauce ma[illegible] follows: 1 cup mayonnaise mixed with 2 table-spoons chopped parsley, 2 tablespoons chopped cucumber, 1 tablespoon capers, and 1 tablespoon anchovy paste. Makes 6 servings.

Sea Stew

Sea stew is similar to cioppino, but easier to serve and eat. If you wish, spoon hot seasoned rice directly into the soup bowls.

1 pound large shrimp or prawns
Boiling salted water
3 dried hot red chiles
1 bay leaf
2½ pounds fish fillets or steaks (rockfish, halibut, seabass, lingcod, or cod)
½ cup flour
½ teaspoon garlic salt
½ teaspoon thyme
2 tablespoons salad oil
2 tablespoons butter
1 medium-sized onion, thinly sliced
1 large can (1 lb., 13 oz.) tomatoes
¾ cup catsup
¾ cup white wine or water
1 whole small lemon, thinly sliced
2 teaspoons sugar
2 teaspoons Worcestershire
Salt and pepper to taste

Cover shrimp with boiling salted water; add chiles and bay leaf and simmer 15 minutes. Strain, saving the cooking liquid for cooking rice, if used; shell shrimp and set aside. Cut fish in large pieces; roll in a mixture of the flour, garlic salt, and thyme. In a frying pan, sauté fish in a combination of the butter and oil until well browned; place in a 2½-quart casserole. Sauté onion in the same pan until soft, about 5 minutes; add tomatoes, catsup, wine, lemon, sugar, Worcestershire, salt, and pepper. Simmer, stirring often, for 15 minutes; add to casserole with shrimp. Cover and bake in moderate oven (350°) for 15 minutes. Makes 6 servings.

SALMON

Fresh and Kippered

Five different species of salmon are caught in the salt and fresh waters of the Pacific Coast, but only two of these species are generally available outside the Pacific Northwest — the king salmon and the silver salmon. One species, the sockeye, is seldom ever found on the fresh market, even in the Northwest.

Each of the salmon may be known by several common names, so the species are easily confused. The king salmon is often called chinook or spring salmon and, in some areas, tyee or blackmouth. This is the largest species, averaging 20 to 25 pounds when mature, and is considered the finest tasting generally available.

The silver salmon may be called coho, silverside, or hooknose. Smaller than the king salmon, it averages 8 to 10 pounds when mature, and is second in importance to the king in the fresh fish market.

Northwest markets sell pink salmon and chum salmon. Sometimes called humpback or humpies, pink salmon average 5 to 6 pounds when mature. They are generally caught only in odd-numbered years and are fine flavored fish if caught in the ocean before they go up the rivers to spawn.

The chum salmon, also known as fall salmon or dog salmon, mature at about 10 to 12 pounds These are generally available from October through December in the Northwest.

The rich meat of salmon is especially delicious barbecued. You can barbecue the whole fish or have it cut into two whole fillets, leaving skin on.

Another good way to cook salmon is to poach it—either the whole fish or a part of it (see opposite page). Then serve the salmon hot with a sauce, or chilled. The poached and chilled fish can also be used to make delicious cold entrées for summer dinners. Poached salmon also goes well in salads and sandwiches and can replace canned salmon in recipes.

Salmon is an excellent fish for baking. The whole fish can be stuffed and baked, and the steaks and fillets lend themselves to a variety of baked entrées (several such recipes are in this chapter).

Using the basic cooking methods described in Chapter I, the steaks from salmon may be broiled, barbecued, poached, or fried.

SMOKED SALMON

Several types of smoked salmon are available. The fanciest is a type called lox. This fish is actually "cooked" in a salt cure, then very lightly smoked. The salmon that results can be sliced wafer thin; it has a buttery richness, subtle salt-smoke flavor, and a bright salmon color.

Other types of smoked salmon are the kippered, mild cure, or Indian type cure. These are drier than lox and usually served in chunks, or flaked for use in a variety of salad and casserole recipes. When you buy smoked salmon, ask about perishability, for it varies considerably with the smoking procedures followed.

Lox is ready to use when purchased, but the drier smoked and kippered salmon may need steaming to soften the texture (directions for steaming follow). Similar to kippered salmon is kippered cod (really sablefish), which is usually less expensive and can be used interchangeably with kippered salmon in many recipes. See page 41 for additional kippered fish recipes.

HOW TO STEAM SMOKED FISH:

Set the piece of fish to be steamed on a rack over boiling water; cover and steam just until heated through. A 1-pound piece of fish takes about 10 to 15 minutes. Either add the hot fish immediately to a hot entrée, or let the steamed fish cool; then chill it for cold dishes.

Poached Salmon (or Seabass) with Shrimp Sauce

To poach a whole salmon or large piece of seabass, you can use a special fish poaching pan (available in shops that handle imported kitchenware) or improvise such a pan. For example, you can poach a fish that will fit in your broiler pan, another large baking pan, or an electric roasting pan.

First prepare the poaching liquid: Double the recipe for the basic poaching liquid on page 7. Cover the pan and simmer the ingredients together slowly for about 30 minutes to 1 hour. Strain and discard whole spices.

To cook the fish: Bring the poaching liquid to a boil in the fish poaching pan over direct heat. Meanwhile, wash a dressed whole salmon (head and tail may be removed), weighing 4-6 pounds, or a 4 to 6-pound piece of white seabass.

Lower the fish into the boiling liquid; wrap fish in cheesecloth for this if you don't have a poaching pan with a special rack. Cover pan; use foil if the pan doesn't have a lid. Simmer either on top of your range or in a hot oven (400°) for 7 to 10 minutes per pound of fish, or until fish flakes easily when pierced with a fork. When done, lift out of liquid and arrange fish on a warm serving plate. Cover with foil and set into a warm oven while you prepare shrimp sauce (recipe follows) or another fish sauce of your choice (see pages 8-11).

To make the shrimp sauce: Set the pan of poaching liquid over high heat and boil rapidly, uncovered, until the liquid is reduced about half (you should have about 2½ cups of the reduced stock). While the broth is boiling, drop into it ½ pound medium-sized fresh shrimp; cook 3 minutes and remove from broth with a slotted spoon. Cool slightly; then peel and devein. Save out a few shrimp for garnish; chop the rest and set aside.

Meanwhile, melt 6 tablespoons butter in another pan. Stir in 6 tablespoons flour and cook until bubbly. Gradually stir in the 2½ cups reduced stock and ½ cup heavy cream. Cook until thickened; add the chopped shrimp. Add salt, if needed.

To serve: Garnish the fish plate with parsley and lemon slices or wedges. Arrange reserved whole shrimp on the fish. Pass the hot shrimp sauce to spoon over each serving. Makes 12 to 18 servings.

Poached Salmon with Cucumber Sauce

For a delicious summertime entrée, poach a 2 to 2½-pound piece of salmon as directed on this page; cool, then chill thoroughly. Serve with a well chilled cucumber sauce: You can make half the recipe for cucumber sauce on page 30, or make sauce Hollandaise with cucumber on page 8.

Poached Salmon with Horseradish Sauce

A piece of fresh salmon, white seabass, or giant sea bass may be poached and served hot or well chilled.

Prepare the basic poaching liquid given on page 7. In a wide frying pan, simmer the ingredients for poaching liquid together for about 15 minutes. Wrap a 2 to 2½-pound piece fresh salmon or seabass in a piece of cheesecloth and lower into the simmering liquid. Cover pan and simmer gently for about 15 minutes, or until fish flakes when tested with a fork. Lift fish out of the liquid and serve hot, or cover and chill. Serve with horseradish sauce (recipe follows). Makes about 6 servings.

To make horseradish sauce: Combine 1 cup sour cream with 1 tablespoon prepared horseradish, ½ teaspoon sugar, ¼ teaspoon salt, dash pepper, ¼ teaspoon grated lemon peel, and 2 teaspoons lemon juice. Chill for at least 1 hour to blend flavors.

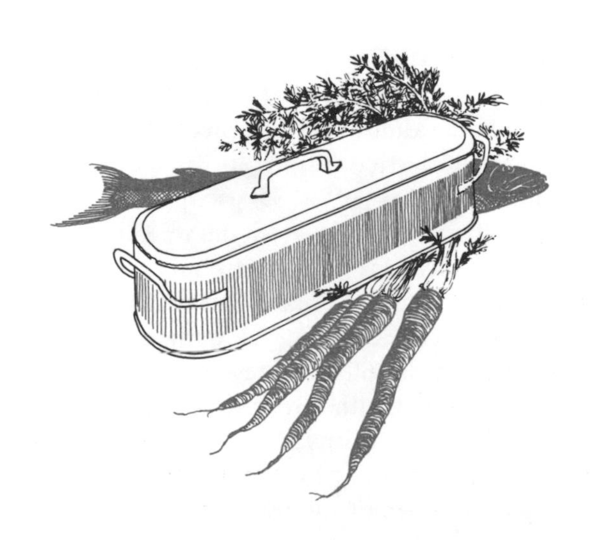

Avocado-Masked Spring Salmon

First oven-poach a whole salmon, about 6 or 7 pounds, in this manner: Remove head and tail; sprinkle inside of salmon with salt. Wrap fish in cheesecloth and place flat in a large baking pan. Add to the pan 1 thinly sliced medium-sized onion, 2 cups dry white table wine, ½ thinly sliced lemon, 1 bay leaf, 1 teaspoon tarragon, 1 teaspoon salt, and 10 whole black peppers. Pour over enough boiling water just to cover fish (about 2 to 3 quarts). Bake in a moderate oven (350°) until thick portion of fish flakes when broken with a fork, about 30 to 40 minutes. Holding fish with cheesecloth, lift from liquid and drain on rack.

While fish is still slightly warm, remove cheesecloth. Carefully pull off skin and remove fins; place on serving tray to chill. Just before serving, spread fish thickly with avocado mask (recipe follows) and decorate with carefully sprinkled minced parsley and lemon slices. Makes 12 servings.

AVOCADO MASK:

With a rotary beater or in a blender, blend smooth 2 medium-sized peeled ripe avocados, 1 can (6 oz.) Hollandaise sauce, ½ teaspoon tarragon, and the juice of 1 lemon or lime. Makes about 2 cups.

Baked Stuffed Salmon

The lemon rice stuffing given in the recipe for Barbecued Salmon, on page 31, is delicious baked inside a whole salmon or large piece of salmon.

Prepare lemon rice stuffing as directed on page 31. Fill the cavity of a 3 to 5-pound dressed salmon with the stuffing. Sew the opening closed with a heavy thread. Place the fish in a well greased baking pan. Arrange 4 bacon slices over the top of the fish. Bake, uncovered, in a moderate oven (350°) for 45 to 60 minutes, or until the fish flakes when tested with a fork; baste several times with drippings or with melted butter. Remove thread before serving. Makes 6 to 10 servings, depending on the size of the fish.

Barbecued Salmon Fillets

A covered barbecue is ideal for barbecuing a whole salmon fillet. If you don't have a covered barbecue, you can shape a hood of foil over the fish to catch some of the smoke of the fire. Have the salmon cut into two whole fillets, leaving the skin on. If you bring home a whole salmon, see pages 53-54 for directions on how to fillet it.

Prepare a baste of ¼ cup melted butter and ¼ cup lemon juice. Have ready 2 whole salmon fillets (from about an 8-pound fish, whole weight). Cut 2 pieces of heavy foil about the same size as the fillets and place against skin side of fish; lay on grill, skin sides down. Cover the barbecue and cook over slow coals until the fish flakes when tested, about 25 minutes (shorter time if fire is hotter). Baste fish several times as it cooks with the butter and lemon juice.

When fish is done, lift each foil lined fillet to a serving plate or plank. To serve, cut the salmon across fillets and just to the skin; lift each serving away from skin. Serve with cucumber sauce (recipe follows) or with additional lemon butter baste or other favorite fish sauce (see pages 8-11).

CUCUMBER SAUCE:

Peel 3 long, thin cucumbers; split into quarters, discard seeds. Finely chop. Sprinkle with 2 teaspoons salt and chill for at least 2 hours; drain well. Mix with 1 cup commercial sour cream, 1 cup mayonnaise, and 1 tablespoon dill weed or chopped fresh dill.

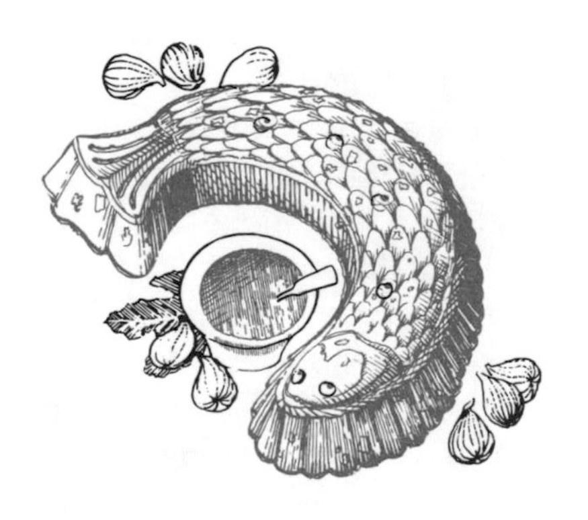

Barbecued salmon with lemon rice stuffing is kept warm on an electrically heated tray. Garnish the fish with grapefruit slices and serve with new potatoes, dill butter, zucchini, tomatoes, and cucumbers.

Barbecued Salmon with Lemon Rice Stuffing

If you don't have a covered barbecue, wrap the salmon in foil; turn it from side to side as it cooks.

LEMON RICE STUFFING:

Heat 1/3 cup butter or margarine in a frying pan. Add 1 cup sliced celery, 1 small onion (chopped), and 1 to 2 cups sliced fresh mushrooms (optional); sauté about 5 minutes. Add 1/4 teaspoon monosodium glutamate, 1/4 teaspoon thyme, 1 1/2 teaspoons salt, 1/8 teaspoon pepper, 2 teaspoons grated lemon peel, 1/4 cup lemon juice, and 1 1/3 cups water. Bring to a boil. Mix in 1 3/4 cups packaged precooked rice and cover; remove from heat; let stand 5 minutes. Makes enough for an 8-pound fish.

TO COOK THE SALMON:

Fill the cavity of a 3 to 8-pound salmon with the lemon rice stuffing. Sew the opening closed with a heavy thread (any stuffing that doesn't fit into the fish can be wrapped in foil and heated on the grill while the fish cooks). If your barbecue has a hood, shape a piece of heavy foil to fit around bottom of fish; grease the foil. Cut very thin slices from a small, thin-skinned grapefruit; place against skin on both sides of fish; then set fish on greased foil. Put on grill over low heat; cover grill. Baste with a little melted butter several times while fish cooks. If your grill doesn't have a hood, wrap the grapefruit-covered fish in double-thick foil. Set it over slowly burning coals (or set the grill as high as possible above coals), and turn about every 10 minutes. Time required is usually about 1 hour. A 4-pound salmon makes about 8 servings.

Salmon Steaks Baked in Lemon Cream

This simple method of baking fish steaks in cream complements other fish as well; try it with white seabass or lingcod steaks.

Arrange 3 or 4 salmon steaks (about 2 pounds) in a buttered baking dish (1½ quart). Pour over top a mixture of 1 cup heavy cream, 5 teaspoons lemon juice, 1 tablespoon minced onion, and ⅛ teaspoon salt. Bake, uncovered, in a hot oven (400°) for about 25 minutes, or until fish flakes easily. Serve with some of the thick cream sauce spooned over each steak. Makes 3 or 4 servings.

Salmon with Oysters

Fresh salmon is baked here in a tomato and green pepper sauce with an accompaniment of oysters.

1 piece fresh salmon (about 3 lbs.)
Salt
2 tablespoons butter
1 tablespoon flour
½ teaspoon freshly ground black pepper
1 cup catsup
1 cup dry white wine
2 teaspoons Worcestershire
1 teaspoon dry mustard
2 tablespoons finely chopped green pepper
1 pint fresh oysters, drained
Watercress (optional)
Lemon slices (optional)
Toast points (optional)

Sprinkle the salmon lightly with salt. Place in a greased, shallow baking dish, preferably a dish you can serve from. Dot surface with butter and sprinkle with flour and black pepper. Bake, uncovered, in a hot oven (400°) for 15 minutes.

In the meantime, combine the catsup, wine, Worcestershire, dry mustard, and green pepper. Remove fish from oven and pour over the catsup mixture. Reduce oven heat to 350°; return salmon to oven and bake 30 minutes more, or until fish flakes easily with a fork. Baste often with sauce. Arrange the drained oysters around the salmon and bake an additional 5 minutes, or until oyster edges curl. Garnish serving dish with watercress and lemon slices, if you wish. To serve individual portions, arrange salmon servings on plates with a few oysters laid on a small piece of toast; spoon sauce over all. Makes 6 servings.

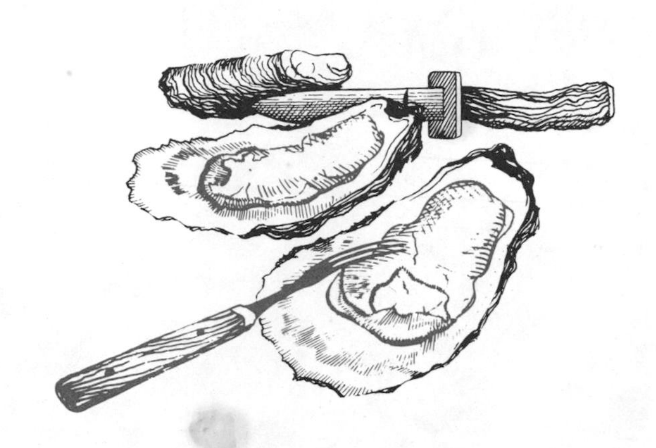

Salmon Steaks with Grapefruit

Grapefruit adds a piquant flavor to salmon steaks, baked crisp with buttered crumbs. If possible, use a heatproof dish that is handsome enough to go directly from the oven to the dinner table.

1 small onion, thinly sliced
6 tablespoons butter or margarine
1 cup soft bread crumbs
½ teaspoon salt
¼ teaspoon pepper
¼ teaspoon allspice
4 salmon steaks, fresh or frozen and defrosted
1 medium-sized grapefruit
About 1 tablespoon chopped parsley
4 thin slices toast (optional)

Lightly sauté onion in 3 tablespoons of the butter. Stir in bread crumbs, salt, pepper, and allspice; remove from heat. Arrange salmon steaks in a well-buttered shallow baking pan. Cut peel and all white membrane from grapefruit; lift out the sections, saving any juice. Pour grapefruit juice over fish; then spoon onion-crumb mixture evenly over fish. Put into a very hot oven (450°) for 10 minutes. Remove fish from oven; arrange grapefruit sections on top of fish and baste with remaining 3 tablespoons butter, melted. Continue baking in a moderately hot oven (375°), basting several more times until browned and tender, about 15 minutes longer. Sprinkle with parsley and serve on toast, if you wish. Makes 4 servings.

Oven-Fried Salmon

Dip salmon into egg and cracker crumbs, and instead of frying it on top of the range, let it cook brown and crisp in the oven, unattended. This same recipe may be used for fillets and steaks of white seabass, halibut, or rockfish; baking time may be less, depending on the thickness of the fish pieces.

2 eggs
1 tablespoon lemon juice
2 tablespoons milk
1 teaspoon salt
1 cup cracker crumbs
1½ pounds salmon steaks or serving-sized fillets
4 tablespoons butter or margarine

Beat eggs slightly; add lemon juice, milk, and salt, and beat until blended. Spread cracker crumbs on a shallow pan or piece of waxed paper. Dip each piece of fish first into egg mixture, then into crumbs; shake off extra crumbs and dip again into egg mixture, then crumbs.

Meanwhile, melt butter in a shallow baking pan (about 8 by 12 inches). Arrange fish in pan, turning each piece to butter both sides. Bake, uncovered, in a moderately hot oven (375°) for 30 to 35 minutes. Serve with wedges of lemon, if you wish. Makes 4 to 6 servings.

Gravlax with Mustard Sauce

Swedish gravlax produces a delicacy similar to the lox you can buy. The fish is actually "cooked" in a salt cure. You might serve it for a luncheon entrée or with a cold buffet.

1 salmon fillet (about 4 lbs.)
¼ cup salad oil
2 tablespoons sugar
1 tablespoon salt
1 teaspoon crushed white pepper
3 teaspoons dill weed or finely chopped fresh dill
Fresh dill leaves or additional weed
Salad oil
Mustard sauce (recipe follows)

Start with the freshest salmon possible; all the bones should be removed, but leave the skin on. Wipe all over with a clean cloth dipped in the ¼ cup salad oil. Combine the sugar, salt, pepper, and 3 teaspoons dill weed or fresh dill (if fresh dill is used, use only the tender leaves). Rub into the fish on all sides. Place the fish in a dish that is as close as possible to the size of the fish. If you have fresh dill leaves, sprinkle them generously in the pan and over the fish; otherwise, use about 2 teaspoons additional dill weed. Cover with a plank or something to exert slight pressure on the fish. Refrigerate 15 to 20 hours, turning it once or twice.

To serve, cut in slices or 1-inch-thick portions. Cut the skin from each portion, including a little of the flesh. Dip these strips of skin in salad oil and fry, skin side down, in a hot, dry frying pan. Serve them hot with the cold fish slices and accompany with mustard sauce. Makes about 12 servings.

MUSTARD SAUCE:

This sauce is good with gravlax. Combine 2 tablespoons sugar and 2 tablespoons mild prepared mustard (you might use imported Swedish mustard), and 3 tablespoons wine vinegar. Gradually add ¾ cup salad oil, whipping vigorously as if making mayonnaise. Stir in 1 teaspoon lemon juice and 1 teaspoon dill weed; season to taste with salt and pepper.

Kedgeree

Kippered salmon is used in kedgeree, a famous English breakfast dish which makes a fine summer supper casserole or Sunday brunch dish.

½ cup wild rice, washed thoroughly
2½ cups water
1 teaspoon salt
½ cup regular long grain rice
5 tablespoons butter or margarine
½ teaspoon curry powder (or more, if desired)
2 tablespoons flour
1 bottle (8 oz.) clam juice
¾ pound kippered salmon
3 hard-cooked eggs
½ cup finely chopped parsley

Soak wild rice in cold water for 1 hour; drain. Bring the 2½ cups water to a boil; add salt, wild rice, and regular rice; cover and simmer 25 to 30 minutes or just until tender. Melt 3 tablespoons of the butter; heat until bubbly and pour over rice mixture; mix with a fork. Melt remaining 2 tablespoons butter; blend in curry powder and flour and gradually stir in clam juice. Cook, stirring, until thickened.

Steam salmon as directed on page 28; then flake and reserve several pieces for garnish. Add the flaked salmon to the rice mixture. Pour the sauce over salmon and rice and mix lightly. Turn into a buttered 2-quart casserole. Halve eggs and separate yolks from whites. Press yolks through a wire strainer and place in a row across the top. Finely chop the whites and place along one side. Arrange parsley in a strip along the other side of the yolks. Garnish with reserved salmon and serve at once. (To reheat, cover and place in a pan of hot water and heat in a moderate oven—350°—for 20 minutes.) Makes 4 to 6 servings.

Swedish Salmon Bowl

Use a large shallow oval bowl for this kippered salmon salad. Arrange the ingredients in stripes; then mix before guests.

1 head iceberg lettuce
1 head romaine
¾ pound kippered salmon, steamed and chilled
⅓ pound fresh mushrooms
1 large avocado
Juice of ½ lemon
3 hard-cooked eggs, sliced
½ pound bacon, cooked and crumbled
1 jar (6 oz.) marinated artichoke hearts
¼ cup olive oil
¼ cup white wine vinegar
½ teaspoon salt
½ teaspoon dry mustard

Tear greens into bite-sized pieces and place in the bottom of a large salad bowl. Flake the salmon (previously steamed as directed on page 28, and chilled) and arrange in a row across the center of the bowl. Wash and slice raw mushrooms and arrange in a row next to the salmon on one side. Peel and slice avocado; dip in lemon juice and arrange along the other side of the fish. Place sliced eggs and crumbled bacon in rows alongside. Drain marinade from the artichokes; reserve marinade and place the artichokes along the other side.

To make the salad dressing, blend the olive oil and wine vinegar into the reserved artichoke marinade and season with salt and mustard; shake well. Pour dressing over salad and mix just before serving. Makes 6 to 8 servings.

Bagels and Lox

Simplicity keynotes a lox sandwich—bland, chewy doughnut-shaped buns with rich, buttery fish and cheese. Accompany it with such juicy relishes as dill pickles, cherry tomatoes, and olives.

6 bagels
1 large package (8 oz.) cream cheese
¾ pound sliced smoked salmon (lox)

Slice bagels horizontally and spread each half with a layer of cream cheese. Place 3 or 4 slices salmon between each sandwich. Makes 6 servings.

UNIQUE AND FATTER FISH

Barracuda, Sablefish, Shad, Sturgeon, Swordfish, Albacore

Often in the realm of fish cookery, pronounced flavor goes hand in hand with moderately high fat content, and this rule holds true for the majority of the fish grouped in this chapter. Most of them are fatter fish, but the range is wide: sturgeon, with about 2 per cent fat, qualifies as very low in fat content; while, at the other extreme, sablefish has about 14 per cent fat, ranking it with salmon.

Frequently quite meat-like in texture, all these fish have marked, rich flavors with two exceptions — sablefish and shad. Sablefish and shad are mild in flavor even though high in fat. And the other fish in the chapter are also unique in one way or another. For this reason, you will need to understand the peculiarities of each one in order to know what special handling or cooking technique is required to prepare it to best advantage.

BARRACUDA

This long, slender fish is sold in Southern California markets throughout the year, with heaviest landings in spring and summer. Barracuda is something like dark-meat tuna in flavor and texture. Its pronounced flavor takes well to robust seasonings, and it is an excellent fish to barbecue.

Most of the barracuda sold in markets are 4 to 7 pounds in size, but may be in the form of steaks or chunks. If you buy a whole fish, it is easy to cut it into steaks ¾ to 1 inch thick. The fish will have less strong flavor if you cut away the dark line on each side under the skin. Barbecue or broil the barracuda steaks or fillets using the basic cooking directions in the first chapter.

SABLEFISH

This little known fish is plentiful along the entire Pacific Coast; you'll find it in markets labeled quite consistently as black cod or butterfish, but rarely by its real name. Because it is a fat fish, it is especially good smoked (or kippered). Most markets carry smoked sablefish, but under the name of smoked black cod or smoked Alaska cod; it can be used in most of the same ways you would use smoked (or kippered) salmon. Some recipes for its use are included in this chapter; also see the kippered salmon recipes on page 34.

The fresh fish has an unusual soft, buttery texture. Take care not to overcook it, for it cooks very quickly. The extremely mild flavor is complemented best by quite tart sauces or bastes. You can barbecue or poach sablefish quite successfully, following the special recipes on pages 40-41. In addition, you might broil sablefish steaks as directed in the first chapter, on page 6.

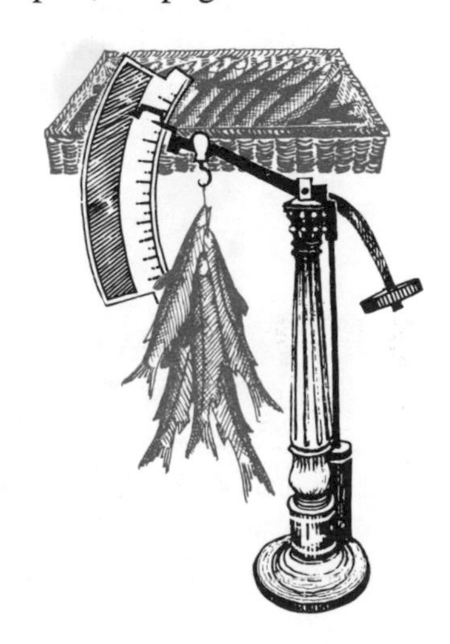

SHAD

Shad is especially bony, but has a delicious meat-like flavor. It is sold in markets only in the Northwest, coming mostly out of the Columbia River. Since it is difficult to fillet, shad is usually sold whole. Baking is the most satisfactory method of cooking the whole fish.

The season for shad is usually March through May in the Northwest. If you happen to buy a roe shad, you'll have an extra delicacy to take home. You can use the roe as a stuffing when you bake shad (see recipe on page 42), or the shad roe may be cooked separately. Shad roe is available in many markets throughout the West during its season in spring; recipes for cooking it are on pages 42-43.

STURGEON

Two species, white sturgeon and green sturgeon are found in Northwest markets. The white sturgeon, larger and more choice, is caught mostly on the Columbia River; these fish have been known to weigh 1,800 pounds, but now it is uncommon to catch one over 500 pounds. Almost depleted in the late 1800's because of the demand for its caviar, sturgeon has been increasing in recent years.

Sturgeon is a lean fish, but quite rich in flavor, compact and meat-like in texture. It is sold in thick steaks or boneless chunks where available. Cook it in the same ways as salmon; like salmon, it is especially good barbecued. Using the basic cooking methods given in the first chapter, you can barbecue, broil, or oven-fry sturgeon steaks.

Northwest markets, especially in the Columbia River area, sell smoked (or kippered) sturgeon, which you can use like kippered salmon or cod (see recipes on pages 34 and 41).

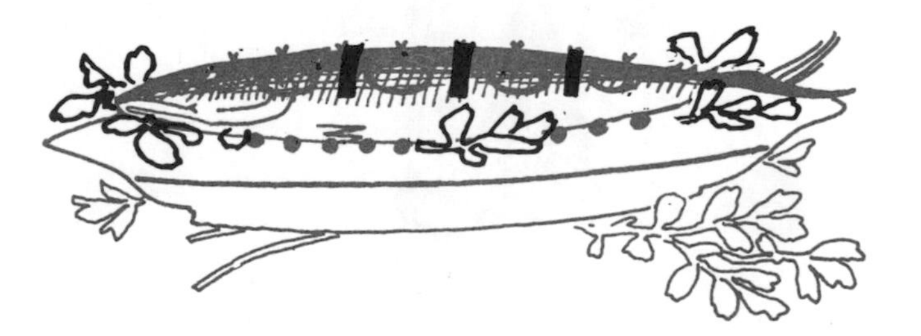

SWORDFISH

The season for these mighty fish lasts only from about July until the last of October. During the rest of the year, only frozen swordfish steaks are available. Southern California markets have the fresh fish when in season, and a little of it comes into Northern California markets; other areas of the West have only the frozen fish.

Fresh swordfish is more expensive than frozen and more difficult to find, even in areas where it is available. But those who savor this excellent fish with meat-like taste consider it well worth the price and extra effort needed to find the fresh fish. Sometimes in coastal markets in Southern California, you can buy a piece of swordfish flank (or belly). While this cut is not as attractive as a steak, it has more fat and is more tender. It is especially good for barbecuing, either cut into kebabs or portion-sized pieces.

Frozen swordfish are often thawed before they are displayed in fresh fish markets; these steaks should *not* be refrozen at home. Use fresh or thawed frozen swordfish steaks interchangeably in the recipes given in this chapter; in addition, you can barbecue, broil, or oven-fry swordfish steaks using the basic cooking directions in the first chapter.

ALBACORE

Albacore is a member of the tuna family. This small, choice, white-meat fish is the only one of the tunas generally available in fresh fish markets. Usually plentiful all along the Pacific coast in summer, it is in demand at tuna canneries; yet few markets carry it regularly.

Your fish dealer can order an albacore for you during its season if you give him a few days' notice; a whole fish weighing 10 to 15 pounds is common. A 12-pound albacore will yield about 8 pounds of nearly solid meat, but if this is more than you can use at once, try one of these suggestions:

Cut the whole fish into thick steaks (see page 37); wrap well and freeze what you don't use the first day. For best flavor plan to use the frozen steaks within a few weeks.

Another possibility is to cut off the number of steaks you can use immediately and poach the rest of the fish to use within the next few days.

A third idea is to poach the whole fish; any meat that you can't use within a few days may be wrapped for short term freezer storage (poaching instructions on this page).

Albacore steaks are particularly delicious barbecued; like salmon, they are enhanced by smoke flavor. The thick steaks also work well for sautéing in a frying pan with sauces for quick entrées.

If you like canned tuna, you'll enjoy poached fresh tuna even more. Once you have poached a whole fish, or part of one, you'll have generous amounts of the meat to use for salads and sandwiches, or in any way you might use canned tuna. The solid piece of poached, well chilled albacore makes a good cold entrée (see page 38).

HOW TO PREPARE ALBACORE STEAKS

An albacore is an especially messy fish to clean, so when you buy it, ask your fish dealer to trim, clean, scale, and cut the fish into inch-thick steaks. But if your fish comes to you whole, it is not difficult to clean it and prepare the steaks yourself.

1) Cover the counter next to your sink with newspapers. Have ready a sharp, heavy knife or cleaver, and a coping saw.

2) First cut off the head, angling the knife from behind the long side fin and using the saw to cut through the backbone; eviscerate the fish.

3) Cut off tail and fins and put the fish in the sink. Scrape off scales and wash well.

4) Place the fish back on the counter and cut it crosswise into inch-thick slices with the knife, using the saw to cut through the center bone.

5) You'll notice that albacore steaks have distinct areas of dark, red meat on each side of the bone. Strong fish oils are concentrated in these areas, so if you simply cut them out before cooking the meat, the flavor will be milder. Use a small sharp knife to cut around and lift out these dark areas; while you're at it, lift out the bone as well.

6) Albacore meat is soft when raw, so your steak may look as though you've ruined it; but don't be concerned. Push the steak back together; if any small pieces have fallen off, poke them into the center.

7) If you plan to barbecue the steak, cut off the skin; wrap a strip of bacon around the outside and secure it with a toothpick. The bacon adds good flavor and holds the piece neatly on the grill.

8) If you'll be sautéing the steak, leave the skin on and use 3 or 4 picks to hold the pieces together. The biggest steaks are best cut into 2 servings each; either wrap each half with bacon or secure sections with picks. Just as soon as the fish begins to cook, the meat firms and welds into neat, easy-to-handle pieces.

HOW TO PREPARE ALBACORE FOR POACHING

The term "loin" is used to describe the boneless section of solid white meat from albacore. The easiest and quickest way to poach albacore is to separate the loins before you poach them, especially if you ask your fish dealer to trim, clean, and fillet the fish for you. Follow these directions for cutting the loins:

1) Carefully pull the skin off each fillet, using a knife when needed to free it from the soft flesh.

2) Cut each fillet in half, lengthwise, along the bone and remove the center bone.

3) You will see streaks of dark red meat running the length of the fillets. With a small sharp knife, cut out and discard dark red portions.

4) Poach the loins as directed below.

HOW TO POACH ALBACORE LOINS

1) Prepare the albacore loins as directed above. Arrange them in a large pan (or your broiler pan) that is at least 2 inches deep.

2) Prepare poaching liquid by combining in another pan 1 quart water, ½ cup vinegar, 2 teaspoons salt, 1 bay leaf, 1 medium-sized onion (stuck with 3 or 4 whole cloves), 1 cut carrot, and 2 sprigs parsley. Heat to simmering and pour over the fish pieces.

3) Cover the pan of fish tightly, using heavy foil, and put it into a hot oven (400°) for about 20 minutes. Remove from oven and carefully lift the loins out of the poaching liquid; cool and chill.

Poached Albacore with Cucumber Sauce

The whole poached loins from an average-sized albacore (about 12 lbs.) make a fine cold entrée for a summer buffet; for family-sized proportions, prepare just ⅓ of the cucumber sauce to use on part of a poached loin section.

Poach albacore loins (about 12 lbs. whole weight) as directed on page 37; chill. Arrange the whole loins side-by-side on a serving tray. Sprinkle with minced parsley or dill and garnish with strips of pimiento, if you wish. Serve with cucumber sauce (recipe follows). Makes about 25 servings.

CUCUMBER SAUCE:

Peel 3 long, thin cucumbers; split into quarters, discard seeds, and finely chop. Sprinkle with 2 teaspoons salt and chill for at least 2 hours; drain well. Mix with 1 cup sour cream, 1 cup mayonnaise, and 1 tablespoon dill weed or chopped fresh dill.

Curried Albacore Salad

Heap curried albacore salad in a salad bowl and serve with toasted almonds and chutney, or make it into individual stuffed tomato salads for a main course. You could substitute an equal amount of drained, canned tuna for the albacore.

2 cups flaked, chilled, poached albacore
1 medium-sized cucumber, peeled and sliced
1 green onion, chopped
2 hard-cooked eggs, sliced
¼ cup mayonnaise
2 tablespoons lemon juice
½ teaspoon curry powder
¼ teaspoon salt
Dash of pepper
2 teaspoons chopped chutney
Salad greens
Toasted, slivered almonds (optional)

Combine in a bowl the albacore, cucumber, green onion, and hard-cooked eggs (saving a few egg slices to garnish top, if you wish). Combine the mayonnaise with the lemon juice, curry, salt, pepper, and chutney. Mix lightly with the albacore. Line a serving bowl with the greens and spoon in the salad. Garnish top with the reserved egg slices or toasted almonds. Makes 4 servings.

STUFFED TOMATO SALADS:

Peel 4 large ripe tomatoes; slice into wedges, cutting from tops to within about ½ inch of the bottom. Set each tomato on an individual salad plate, spreading wedges apart; sprinkle with salt and pepper to taste. Prepare the albacore mixture as above and spoon into the tomatoes. Garnish each serving with an egg slice. Makes 4 servings.

Albacore with Sour Cream Sauce

Sour cream with capers complements sautéed albacore steaks.

6 serving-sized pieces albacore steak
¼ cup butter, margarine, or salad oil
Salt and pepper to taste
1 medium-sized onion, sliced
1 cup sour cream
2 tablespoons chopped capers

Prepare the steaks as directed on page 37; do not wrap in bacon. Heat the butter, margarine, or oil in a large frying pan. Sauté the steaks over medium heat until nicely browned and they test done with a fork, sprinkling with salt and pepper to taste. Remove fish to a serving plate and keep warm. In the same pan, sauté the onion until lightly browned. Reduce heat and stir in the sour cream and capers; heat through and pour over the sautéed steaks. Makes 6 servings.

Albacore in Tomato Sauce

Tomato is one of the most successful flavors with albacore. Use your electric frying pan or any frying pan with a tight cover to sauté these fish steaks.

6 serving-sized pieces albacore steak
1/3 cup olive oil or salad oil
1 teaspoon salt
Dash of pepper
1 medium-sized onion, sliced
1 can (8 oz.) tomato sauce
3/4 cup white wine
1 bay leaf
1 tablespoon chopped parsley
1 teaspoon sugar
1/2 teaspoon thyme

Prepare the fish steaks as described on page 37; do not wrap pieces in bacon. Heat the oil in a large frying pan; add the fish, sprinkle it with the salt and pepper, and sauté quickly until browned on both sides. Remove the fish from the pan; set aside. In the same heated fat, sauté the onion until soft. Add the tomato sauce, wine, bay leaf, parsley, sugar, and thyme. Simmer 5 minutes. Add the browned fish slices to the pan, cover, and cook 5 to 10 minutes, or until it tests done with a fork. Remove the fish to a serving plate, pour the sauce around it, and sprinkle with more chopped parsley, if you wish. Makes 6 servings.

Barbecued Albacore with Lemon Butter

Take your choice of ways to barbecue these fish steaks; each uses the same basting sauce.

6 serving-sized pieces albacore steak
6 slices bacon (optional)
1/2 cup (1/4 lb.) butter
1 medium-sized clove garlic, minced or mashed
4 tablespoons lemon juice
2 tablespoons chopped parsley
Salt and pepper to taste

Prepare the albacore steaks as described on page 37 (they may be plain or wrapped with bacon). For the basting sauce, melt the butter in a small pan; stir in the garlic, lemon juice, and parsley. Have ready a good bed of medium-hot coals in the barbecue; grease the grill and arrange the steaks on it. Cook a total of 10 to 15 minutes, turning once, and brushing several times with the baste; sprinkle with salt and pepper to taste. Makes 6 servings.

SMOKE-BARBECUED ALBACORE:

Arrange albacore steaks on the grill on a piece of heavy foil with holes poked in it. Cover the barbecue and adjust the drafts for slow cooking. Cook 20 to 30 minutes, depending on heat of your fire. Remove cover several times to brush with the basting sauce, but don't turn the fish. Salt and pepper to taste.

OYSTER-TOPPED ALBACORE:

Prepare the steaks as for smoke-barbecuing. Top each steak with several thin slices of sweet onion, 1 thin slice of a large tomato, 1 or 2 Pacific oysters, and 1 thin lemon slice. Smoke-barbecue as above, brushing several times with the basting sauce. Salt and pepper to taste.

Sesame-Soy Barbecued Albacore

Sesame seed toasts on each side of teriyaki-flavored albacore steaks.

4 to 6 serving-sized pieces albacore steak
4 or 6 bacon slices (optional)
4 tablespoons (1/8 lb.) butter
3 tablespoons soy sauce
2 tablespoons lemon juice
2 tablespoons sherry
2 to 3 teaspoons sesame seed

Prepare the albacore steaks as described on page 37 with or without bacon wrapping. In a small pan, melt the butter and stir in the soy sauce, lemon juice, and sherry. Arrange the steaks on a greased grill; brush fish well with the baste and barbecue over medium-hot coals for a total of 10 to 15 minutes cooking time. When the steaks are half done, brush tops with baste; sprinkle with sesame seed, using about 1/4 teaspoon on each steak and turn over. Cook until browned on the second side and brush tops again with baste; sprinkle with more sesame seed and turn back to the first side long enough to toast the seed. Makes 4 to 6 servings.

Barbecued Barracuda

Cut about 3 pounds barracuda into steaks, each about 3/4 inch thick. Prepare either basil-garlic baste (see page 44) or teriyaki sauce (page 24, under "Rockfish in Foil"). Pour either sauce over the fish in a bowl and marinate for 10 minutes.

Remove fish from marinade and set on the grill on top of a piece of heavy foil (with holes punched in it), or hold the fish pieces in a hinged wire broiler over the fire. Cook over medium-hot coals, turning and basting with the sauce as needed, for 8 to 10 minutes, or until fish flakes easily.

Barracuda Casserole

Cut about 2 pounds barracuda meat from bones in large chunks, and put into a well greased 1 1/2-quart casserole. Combine 1/2 cup chopped sweet onion with 1 canned pimiento, chopped, 1 can (8 oz.) tomato sauce, 1 teaspoon oregano, 1 teaspoon salt, and dash of pepper. Pour over fish and mix in lightly. Cover and bake in a moderately hot oven (375°) for about 30 minutes, or until fish flakes easily. Spoon some of the sauce over fish when serving. Makes 4 to 6 servings.

Sablefish Poached in Tart Broth

Fresh sablefish steaks are delicious poached in a tart broth.

1 quart water
1 cup white wine vinegar
1 tablespoon salt
1/2 teaspoon sugar
4 whole black peppers
4 whole allspice
1 bay leaf
1/2 medium-sized onion, sliced
About 3 pounds fresh sablefish steaks

To make the broth, combine in a large frying pan the water, white wine vinegar, salt, sugar, whole black peppers, allspice, bay leaf and onion. Bring to a boil. Wrap fish steaks in cheesecloth and carefully set into broth, one piece at a time, letting broth return each time to simmering. Remove from heat; let stand 5 minutes, or until fish flakes easily. (Be careful not to overcook this fish.) Remove fish to a warm plate and serve with melted butter, flavored with chopped parsley. Makes 6 servings.

Barbecued Sablefish

Sablefish is a good choice for the barbecue when prepared this way. Have it cut into two whole fillets, leaving the skin on.

¼ cup melted butter or margarine
1 cup lemon juice
1 cup sherry or dry vermouth
2 sablefish whole fillets (from about 8-pound fish, whole weight), skin left on

Prepare this marinade: Combine melted butter or margarine with lemon juice and sherry or dry vermouth in a pan large enough to hold the fish. Have ready sablefish fillets. Cut 2 pieces of heavy foil about the same size as the fillets and place against skin side of fish; lay on grill, skin sides down. Barbecue over slow coals, for about 25 minutes (shorter time if fire is hotter), preferably on a covered grill; you can shape a hood of foil over the fish to catch some of the smoke of the fire. Baste fish as it cooks. Meanwhile heat the marinade. Let cooked fish stand in the marinade for about 10 minutes before serving. Makes 6 to 8 servings.

Smoked Fish and Egg Bake

Smoked sablefish (kippered cod) is baked in an egg custard for this casserole. It is especially appropriate to serve for lunch.

1 tablespoon chopped parsley
1 tablespoon chopped chives or green onions
1 pound kippered cod or kippered salmon
2 eggs
1 cup milk

Sprinkle the chopped parsley and chopped chives evenly over the bottom of a well greased 1½-quart casserole. Flake the kippered salmon or kippered cod, removing the bones (it needn't be steamed). Spoon the fish into the casserole. Beat together the eggs and milk until will blended and pour over the fish in the casserole. Bake, uncovered, in a moderate oven (350°) for about 35 minutes, or until the custard is set. Makes about 4 servings.

Smoked Fish in Caper Cream Sauce

The flavor of capers blends well with that of kippered sablefish (called kippered cod) or kippered salmon. Try creamed fish for breakfast or brunch.

1 to 1½ pounds kippered cod or kippered salmon
2 tablespoons butter or margarine
2 tablespoons flour
1 cup light cream or half-and-half (half milk, half cream)
1 tablespoon chopped capers
4 prepared patty shells or 4 slices toast

Steam the kippered salmon or kippered cod as directed on page 28. Using two forks, flake into bite-sized pieces while hot, removing the bones. Meanwhile, melt the butter or margarine in a pan; stir in the flour and cook until bubbly. Remove from heat while you slowly stir in the light cream. Add the chopped capers and cook, stirring, until thickened. Stir in the hot fish. Serve in the patty shells or on crisp toast points. Makes 4 servings.

Baked Shad

If you have a roe shad, you may use the roe to stuff the cavity of the fish when you bake it.

Sprinkle cavity of a 5 or 6-pound dressed shad with salt and pepper to taste. Stuff cavity with roe if you wish. Lay 4 slices bacon across rack of broiling pan. Place shad on bacon and lay 4 more slices bacon on top of fish. Bake, uncovered, in a moderately hot oven (375°) for 45 to 50 minutes, or until fish flakes easily. To serve, slice across fish, cutting through the bone. Makes 4 to 6 servings.

Shad Roe Baked in Cream

Here is an easy, yet elegant way to serve shad roe.

1 large set (about ¾ lb.) shad roe
¾ cup heavy cream
¼ teaspoon marjoram
¼ teaspoon chervil
½ teaspoon salt
Dash pepper
1 onion slice, ¼ inch thick
1 bay leaf
2 sprigs parsley

Prepare shad roe as directed below. Arrange shad roe in a generously buttered small baking dish (about 7½ by 5½ inches). Combine heavy cream with marjoram, chervil, salt, and dash of pepper; pour over the roe in the dish. Add to the dish the onion, bay leaf, and parsley. Cover and bake in a moderate oven (350°) for 30 to 40 minutes, or until the roe eggs have turned opaque white throughout. Remove the onion, bay, and parsley, and serve the roe with the cream. Makes 2 servings.

HOW TO PREPARE SHAD ROE FOR COOKING:

The roe of shad is contained in two separate pouches, loosely joined by a thin membrane; they are sold as a set. A fairly large set, weighing about ¾ pound, divides nicely into 2 servings.

Before cooking shad roe, wash it gently, being careful not to break the membrane covering. Pat dry with paper towels. Do not separate the set until after you have cooked it.

Butter-Broiled Shad Roe

An herb-flavored butter mixture is used to season broiled shad roe.

1 large set (about ¾ lb.) shad roe
3 tablespoons butter
1½ tablespoons lemon juice
¼ teaspoon chervil (optional)
Buttered toast points (optional)
1 teaspoon chopped chives
1 teaspoon chopped parsley
Salt and pepper
Crisp bacon (optional)
Lemon wedges (optional)

Prepare shad roe as directed above. Arrange shad roe in a generously buttered broiler pan. Melt butter. Stir in lemon juice and chervil, if desired. Brush the roe with part of this butter and broil about 4 inches below source of heat for about 5 minutes on each side, brushing several times with the butter mixture. Remove to a warm serving plate or serve on buttered toast. Add chives and parsley to the remaining lemon butter and pour over the broiled roe. Salt and pepper to taste. Serve with crisped bacon; offer lemon to squeeze over roe, if you wish. Makes 2 servings.

Pan-Fried Sturgeon

Here is a very simple way to cook and serve fresh sturgeon steaks.

Trim off skin from 2 pounds sturgeon steaks, cut about 1 inch thick. Lightly coat in flour, seasoned with salt and pepper. Sauté in about ⅛ inch salad oil in a large frying pan until it is nicely browned and flakes easily (5 to 8 minutes on each side). Meanwhile, prepare lemon-parsley butter: Melt ¼ cup (⅛ lb.) butter and add the juice of 1 lemon and 1 tablespoon parsley. Serve fish on a warm platter; pour over lemon butter. Makes about 4 servings.

Butter-Sautéed Shad Roe

The simple method of butter-sautéing does not mask the delicate flavor and unique texture of shad roe.

1 large set (about ¾ lb.) shad roe
2 tablespoons flour
¼ teaspoon salt
Dash pepper
2 tablespoons butter
Lemon wedges
Buttered toast points (optional)
Crisp bacon (optional)
1 tablespoon butter (optional)
Minced parsley (optional)

Prepare shad roe as directed on page 42. Combine flour with salt and pepper. Dust shad roe with the flour to coat lightly. Heat the 2 tablespoons butter in a small frying pan over medium heat and sauté the roe until nicely browned on both sides and eggs have become opaque white throughout. (To test, make a slit to the center with a sharp knife.) Serve with lemon wedges to be squeezed over the top. You might arrange each serving on a buttered piece of toast and serve with crisp bacon. Also, if you wish, melt an additional tablespoon butter in the pan until it turns a golden brown, then pour over the sautéed roe and sprinkle with minced parsley. Makes 2 servings.

Pickled Sturgeon

Pickled sturgeon is best after it has stood about a week in the refrigerator, and will keep well to about five weeks.

1 piece sturgeon (2 to 2½ pounds)
1 quart water
3 tablespoons salt
2 cups white wine vinegar
1 cup water
½ cup mild honey
6 to 8 bay leaves or myrtle leaves
1 tablespoon whole cloves
1 tablespoon celery seed
1 tablespoon mustard seed
2 large, sweet onions, thinly sliced

Soak sturgeon overnight in the water mixed with the salt. Drain, remove skin, and cut fish into about 1 by 3-inch pieces. In a pan, bring to a boil white vinegar, water, honey, bay leaves or myrtle leaves, cloves, celery seed, and mustard seed. Drop pieces of fish into boiling brine, and cook just until they turn white throughout, 2 to 3 minutes. Remove fish, cool, and cut into bite-sized pieces. Mix fish with onions; pack into 3 pint jars. Bring the brine to a boil again, cool slightly, and pour over fish in the jars to cover, distributing the spices evenly. Cover and store in the refrigerator. Makes about 3 pints.

Swordfish steaks broiled in Mexican coastal style are garnished with parsley-flecked lemon slices and rolled anchovy fillets. Serve swordfish Sinaloa with avocado salad and crusty dinner rolls.

Broiled Swordfish, Sinaloa

A simple method for broiling swordfish steaks with garlic-butter baste, mustard, and anchovies comes from the Mexican coastal state of Sinaloa.

Heat 2 tablespoons butter and 2 tablespoons lemon juice with 1 clove garlic, minced, until butter is melted. Place 4 swordfish steaks (8 to 10 oz. each), cut ¾ inch thick, on a well greased broiler rack; place in a preheated broiler about 3 inches from heat. Baste with lemon butter. Broil for 6 to 8 minutes or until lightly browned. Turn and rub 1 teaspoon dry mustard into second sides; then sprinkle evenly with 6 flat anchovy fillets, drained and chopped; baste again with lemon butter. Continue broiling until fish is browned and flakes easily when tested with a fork, about 5 minutes longer. Makes 4 servings.

Barbecued Swordfish with Basil-Garlic Baste

Cut about 3 pounds swordfish into ¾-inch-thick steaks or into kebabs. Place in a bowl and pour over them basil-garlic baste (recipe follows); marinate for 5 minutes. Remove fish from marinade and barbecue about 10 minutes (8 minutes for kebabs) over moderately hot coals; turn as needed and brush several times with the baste. Makes 6 to 8 servings.

BASIL-GARLIC BASTE:

Combine 1 cup salad oil, 1 cup white wine vinegar, 1 small clove garlic, mashed, 1 tablespoon parsley, 1 teaspoon salt, ½ teaspoon basil, and ⅛ teaspoon pepper.

Swordfish on Skewer

Bay leaves are placed between cubes of swordfish to add flavor while grilling.

1 tablespoon salad oil or olive oil
1 tablespoon salt
1 tablespoon chopped parsley
¼ teaspoon pepper
Juice of 1 lemon
2 pounds swordfish, cut in 1½-inch pieces
About 20 bay leaves
Oil and lemon sauce (recipe follows)

Combine in a small bowl salad oil or olive oil, salt, parsley, pepper, and lemon juice. Dip swordfish cubes in sauce. Thread fish on skewer, placing a bay leaf between every two pieces of fish. Grill about 4 inches above hot coals for about 5 minutes. Turn and grill 5 minutes on other side. Brush with sauce during grilling. Serve with oil and lemon sauce (recipe follows). Makes 4 servings.

OIL AND LEMON SAUCE:

Mix or shake in a small bowl or jar with lid, 3 tablespoons olive oil, 3 tablespoons lemon juice, 1 tablespoon chopped parsley, 1 teaspoon dry mustard (optional), 1 clove garlic, mashed (optional), and salt and pepper to taste.

Baked Swordfish, Manzanillo

Along the Mexican coast, swordfish is baked in a generous quantity of olive oil with green onions.

Sprinkle 4 swordfish steaks (about 8 oz. each) with 1½ teaspoons salt and ⅛ teaspoon pepper. Place fish in a single layer in a baking dish; brush with 6 tablespoons olive oil to coat heavily. Sprinkle ½ cup sliced green onions over the fish. Bake, uncovered, in a moderate oven (350°) for about 20 minutes or until fish flakes easily with a fork. Remove to platter and serve sprinkled with chopped parsley and garnished with tomato and lime wedges. Makes 4 servings.

Swordfish Stroganoff

Green noodles provide a colorful base for creamy swordfish stroganoff.

3 swordfish steaks (about 1½ lbs.)
¼ cup butter or margarine
1 large, flat, mild onion, thinly sliced
¼ pound mushrooms, sliced
¼ cup dry white wine
1 teaspoon salt
1 teaspoon Worcestershire
2 teaspoons lemon juice
½ teaspoon prepared Dijon-style mustard
Dash pepper
1½ cups sour cream
Buttered, hot, cooked green noodles
Paprika and chopped parsley for garnish

Cut fish into strips about ½ by 2 inches. Heat butter in a heavy frying pan; cook onion until soft, then add mushrooms and stir until limp. Remove onion and mushrooms from pan with a slotted spoon; reserve. Sauté swordfish strips in same pan until white and firm, stirring occasionally to cook on all sides, about 4 minutes. Blend wine, salt, Worcestershire, lemon juice, mustard, and pepper with sour cream until smooth. Return onion and mushrooms to pan with sour cream mixture. Stir gently to blend. Cook just until sour cream is heated through. Serve, sprinkled with paprika and parsley, over green noodles. Makes 4 servings.

PAN-SIZED WHOLE FISH

Mackerel, Smelt, Surfperch, Trout

The small fish discussed in this chapter are usually cooked whole. One large trout, small surfperch, small mackerel, or large jacksmelt makes a serving. Most of the smelt are smaller, so it takes half a dozen or more for a serving. Larger surfperch and mackerel can be split to make two servings.

A wide range of fish flavors is represented in this group — mild surfperch, richly flavored smelt, robustly flavored mackerel. Some of the smallest sole are sold as whole fish; thus these delicately flavored fish may also be cooked by some of the methods described in this chapter.

MACKEREL

Two species of mackerel are caught off the southern Pacific Coast. Pacific mackerel (often called blue or American mackerel) is the most popular and the only one generally available in California markets. Jack mackerel (sometimes called Spanish mackerel) is often caught by sportfishermen, but its flavor is too strong for most tastes.

Pacific mackerel is a member of the tuna family. Its dark meat is moderately high in fat content and pronounced in flavor. Best barbecued or broiled, use the special recipes for mackerel in this chapter (see page 47) or the basic cooking directions in the first chapter. Mackerel is easiest to cook if you have it split and boned at the market.

SMELT

Numerous species of fish are called smelt in our markets. Those called smelt in California actually belong to two different families of fish: silversides and true smelt. Jacksmelt, topsmelt, and grunions are silversides. Surf (or silver) smelt, whitebait, and eulachon are true smelt. The fish of both families are small and fine for eating, although the true smelt are considered superior in flavor. In fat content these fish vary by species and season, but generally true smelt are fatter and richer in flavor than silversides.

In the Northwest, the two important species of smelt are the surf (or silver) smelt and the eulachon (called Columbia River smelt or candlefish). Both are true smelt, but eulachons are richer in fat. These fish are caught as they go up the rivers to spawn; their season is January to April. An interesting feature of the Northwest surf smelt is that they are sometimes sold boned at a small additional price (they're certainly worth the extra cost for anyone who objects to fish bones).

Some of the simplest cooking methods are best for smelt; you can butter-sauté, fry, or oven-fry them following the basic cooking directions in the first chapter. For an interesting variation of butter-sautéed smelt, substitute rye flour for regular flour in the directions given on page 5. Some of the jacksmelt are about the same size as trout and can be substituted for trout in recipes.

SURFPERCH

A number of different species of these small fish are caught in shallow waters along the Pacific Coast. Many are caught by surf fishermen, and some are sold in fresh fish markets. Of the California-caught fish, many people regard the redtail surfperch as the finest for eating.

In Northwest markets, surfperch are commonly called sea perch; they are not to be confused with Pacific Ocean perch, the name widely used for some of the rockfish which are landed in the Northwest and sold filleted, packaged, and frozen in supermarkets throughout the West.

When you buy surfperch at a fresh fish market, it is a good idea to have them trimmed (dressed) and skinned at the market. If you catch your own, see pages 52-53 for directions on how to trim and skin them. The dressed and skinned fish can be fried, oven-fried, or broiled using the basic directions in the first chapter; a special recipe for butter-sautéing surfperch is included in this chapter.

TROUT

The demand for trout by connoisseurs who savor its distinctive flavor has caused more and more trout to be raised on farms for the commercial market. Idaho supplies a large share of the trout market, and many are imported from Japan and Denmark; when sold defrosted, trout shouldn't be refrozen at home.

The trout recipes in this chapter are suitable for freshly caught trout or defrosted frozen trout from the market. The smoke of the barbecue enhances the flavor of this fish and, in addition to barbecuing, it may be butter-sautéed, poached, broiled, or oven-fried by the basic cooking methods described in the first chapter.

Planked Mackerel and Mushroom Caps

A prepared hardwood plank is the traditional way to cook and serve this Italian style fish dish; however, you can also use one of the new broiler pans designed to go directly from the broiler to the table.

If you use a plank, it should be oil seasoned. Before cooking on it, be sure to oil it again; then preheat by placing it in a cold oven; turn the heat to 425° and leave for 15 minutes.

Split lengthwise 3 mackerel (each about 1 lb.). Wash and pat dry. Arrange, cut side down, on a large oil-seasoned hardwood plank or greased broiler pan. Alongside the fish, place 6 large (or 12 medium-sized) mushrooms, stems removed and cap side up. Brush fish and mushrooms with melted butter and sprinkle with salt and pepper. Broil 6 inches below heat for about 12 minutes, or until fish flakes when tested with a fork; baste when needed with more butter. Garnish and serve with lemon wedges. Makes 6 servings.

Barbecued Mackerel

Buy about 1-pound mackerels for barbecuing and have them split and boned at the market.

½ cup dry bread crumbs
½ cup grated Parmesan cheese
2 cloves garlic, mashed
¼ teaspoon salt
Dash pepper
⅓ cup salad oil
⅓ cup lemon juice
1 tablespoon chopped parsley
½ teaspoon basil
4 mackerels (about 1 lb. each), split and boned

Mix dry bread crumbs with Parmesan cheese, 1 clove of the garlic, the salt, and pepper. Also have ready a basting sauce made by combining salad oil and lemon juice with the remaining 1 clove garlic, chopped parsley, and basil. Dip each fish fillet in the basting sauce, then in crumb mixture. Set over slow coals on a greased grill. Cook slowly, turning once and dabbing often with the baste, until the fish flakes (about 15 minutes). Makes 4 servings.

Pickled Smelt Rolls

If you live where boned smelt are available, use them for this recipe; if your smelt are unboned, see the boning directions below.

You might serve these pickled fish for a first course at dinner with thin rye crackers. For a summer lunch, offer the smelt rolls along with an assortment of cheeses and good rye and pumpernickel breads for sandwich making.

1 pound small smelt (12 to 16 per lb.)
1 medium-sized onion, finely chopped
2 teaspoons salt
¼ teaspoon pepper
1 teaspoon dill weed
½ cup white wine vinegar
½ cup dry white wine
1 teaspoon sugar

If you have not bought boneless smelt, remove the heads and tails, and clean smelt. Cut each end to end with scissors; then lift out bone. Combine onion with salt, pepper, and dill weed. Spread on the flesh side of each piece of smelt. Starting at the head end of boned smelt, roll up, enclosing the filling. Arrange the rolls, with open ends down, in an ungreased 1½-quart casserole. Pour over a mixture of the white wine vinegar, dry white wine, and sugar. (Instead of the wine vinegar and wine, you can use ½ cup each of regular white vinegar and water.) Cover and bake in a moderate oven (350°) for 15 to 20 minutes. Cool in liquid, and chill at least 12 hours; or you can keep the pickled smelt in the refrigerator up to 2 weeks. Makes 6 to 8 servings of 2 rolls each.

Butter-Sautéed Surfperch

Have surfperch dressed and skinned for butter-sautéing. Plan on 1 small perch (1 to 1½ lbs.) for each serving. For 4 perch, lightly brown 1 sliced onion in ¼ cup (⅛ lb.) melted butter; remove onion with a slotted spoon and discard. Roll the fish in fine dry bread crumbs (or in wheat germ); sauté in the butter over medium-high heat until browned, about 2 minutes on each side. Salt and pepper lightly to taste. Makes 4 servings.

Butterflied and Barbecued Trout

Boned, butterflied trout marinate in Italian-style dressing, and then are barbecued or broiled; serve them with nut butter.

Bone 4 medium-sized dressed trout as directed below; place in shallow pan and pour about 1½ cups Italian-style oil and vinegar dressing over fish; allow to stand, covered, in refrigerator for about 30 minutes. Remove fish from marinade; place skin side down on barbecue grill or lightly greased broiler pan. Cook for about 10 minutes, or until flesh of trout is white and moist. If you wish, brush occasionally with marinade. Meanwhile, melt ½ cup (¼ lb.) butter or margarine, and add ½ cup chopped salted macadamia nuts; keep warm. Remove trout to heated platter; serve with nut butter. Makes 4 servings.

HOW TO BONE TROUT:

To bone dressed, uncooked trout and keep the head and tail in place, open the body cavity; insert a sharp knife at the head end under the backbone and cut between the ribs and flesh, releasing the bones from the fish back (take care not to cut through the back of the fish). Repeat to free the other side of the backbone and rib cage. Ease backbone free, leaving back flesh of trout intact. Using kitchen scissors, snip backbone at head and tail; lift out the bony skeleton and discard. Cut off and discard fins. Fish is now ready for barbecuing open, or you can stuff it for baking.

Sautéed trout and mushroom caps are embellished with lemon, butter, and cream, blended together in a sauce. Use this recipe for freshly caught trout or defrosted frozen trout from the market.

Mushroom-Stuffed Baked Trout

Bone the trout as directed on page 48. Then fold the boned trout around sautéed mushrooms and bake for this dish.

Melt 2 tablespoons butter in medium-sized frying pan. Add ¼ pound sliced mushrooms, 1 tablespoon chopped green onion, 1 tablespoon chopped parsley, ¼ teaspoon salt, and ¼ teaspoon tarragon. Cook, stirring occasionally, until mushrooms are tender. Rinse 4 medium-sized boned dressed trout; pat dry with paper towel. Sprinkle each lightly with salt and lemon juice. Spoon about 3 tablespoons of the mushroom stuffing into each trout. Fold trout to enclose filling. Wrap each trout with a strip of bacon. Place on broiling pan with a rack; brush each trout with melted butter (you'll need about 1 tablespoon, total). Bake in hot oven (425°) for 10 to 15 minutes, or until fish flakes with fork. Serve with lemon. Makes 4 servings.

Trout in Butter Sauce

Interesting seasonings added to butter-sautéed trout enhance its distinctive flavor.

Select 4 pan-dressed trout, each 8 to 10 inches long; wash and pat dry. Sprinkle inside and out with salt to taste. Roll in flour; shake off excess. Heat ¼ cup (⅛ lb.) butter or margarine in a frying pan (use one that is large enough so that trout lie flat); quickly brown fish on both sides, taking care not to burn. Transfer cooked fish to a warm platter and keep hot.

Place in the frying pan an additional ¼ cup (⅛ lb.) butter or margarine, ½ teaspoon mace, dash freshly ground black pepper, 4 fresh sage leaves (cut in fine strips) or ¼ teaspoon of the dried herb, and the grated peel and juice of 1 lemon. Heat until butter melts and bubbles; pour over trout. Garnish with parsley and lemon slices. Serve immediately. Makes 4 servings.

Sautéed Trout and Mushrooms in Cream

1 cup fresh small mushrooms, or 1 can (3 or 4 oz.) whole mushrooms, drained
1/3 cup butter
1/4 teaspoon salt
3 to 4 medium-sized trout (about 1/2 lb. each), *dressed*
Juice of 1/2 lemon
1/3 cup whipping cream

Sauté mushrooms in the butter in a large frying pan for about 5 minutes. (If using canned mushrooms, just heat through.) Remove to a warm platter. Add salt to the remaining butter; add fish and sauté about 3 minutes per side. Remove the sautéed fish to the platter. Quickly stir in the lemon juice; add the cream and stir just until heated through. Spoon immediately over the fish and mushrooms, and serve. Makes 3 to 4 servings.

Brazilian Baked Trout

Fresh trout baked in wine is a delicious entrée for a guest meal.

4 to 6 medium-sized trout (about 1/2 lb. each), pan-dressed
Juice of 1 lemon
1 teaspoon salt
1 clove garlic, minced or mashed
1 cup dry white wine
2 tablespoons chopped parsley
2 tablespoons green onion rings
2 tablespoons dry bread crumbs
4 tablespoons melted butter

Wash and dry trout with paper towels; rub outside with lemon juice and sprinkle with salt. Arrange the minced garlic in the bottom of a buttered, shallow baking dish large enough to hold trout in a single layer. Place trout in dish; pour wine over top. Sprinkle the parsley, green onion, and dry bread crumbs over trout; then spoon on butter. Bake, uncovered, in a hot oven (400°) for 20 minutes. Serve hot. Makes 4 to 6 servings.

Oven-Crisp Trout

6 trout, pan-dressed
Salt and pepper
1/4 cup (4 tablespoons) soft butter
1/2 cup finely chopped parsley
1 egg
1/4 cup milk
1 teaspoon salt
3/4 cup fine dry bread crumbs, toasted
1/2 cup shredded Swiss cheese
2 tablespoons butter

Wash trout and pat dry with paper towels. Sprinkle inside the fish lightly with salt and pepper. Combine the butter and parsley and spread the mixture inside the cavity of each fish. Beat the egg together with the milk and salt. Also have ready the bread crumbs combined with the cheese. Dip each fish in the egg mixture and roll in the crumb-cheese mixture to coat each side well. Arrange the fish on a generously buttered shallow baking pan. If any of the crumb mixture is left, sprinkle it over the tops of the fish; dot with the 2 tablespoons butter. Bake in a very hot oven (500°) for 15 to 20 minutes, or until fish are tender and browned. Makes 6 servings.

Chilled Trout with Dill Sauce

First poach your trout as directed under "How to Poach Fish," on page 7 of the first chapter, using the basic poaching liquid on that page. Have the fish well chilled before serving.

2 medium-sized or 4 small trout, poached and chilled
Parsley sprigs and lemon wedges
1/2 cup sour cream
2 teaspoons lemon juice
1/2 teaspoon salt
1/4 teaspoon dill weed

Arrange the trout on a serving dish; garnish with parsley sprigs and lemon wedges. Make the sauce by mixing together the sour cream, lemon juice, salt, and dill weed. Serve sauce from a small serving bowl. Makes 2 to 4 servings.

SPORTSMAN'S CATCH

Bonito, Sheepshead, Kelp Bass, Sand Bass, Striped Bass

The way you cook a fish naturally depends upon what type of fish it is. For the most part, fish that are caught along the ocean shores and from party fishing boats that go out from the coastal ports are the same fish that are sold in markets: Salmon, rockfish, sablefish, and lingcod are commonly caught by sportfishermen all along the Pacific Coast; barracuda, albacore, and other tunas are taken primarily along the southern part of the Coast; surfperch and sole (or flounder) are taken in the shallow coastal waters. Methods of cooking these fish are discussed in detail in the earlier chapters of the book (see index).

But some other ocean fish are also worth saving and eating; these include bonito, kelp bass, sand bass, and sheepshead. These are discussed in this chapter, along with one fish delicacy reserved for the sportfisherman — striped bass. (Trout recipes are given on pages 47-50.)

PACIFIC BONITO

A member of the tuna family, Pacific bonito ranges in size up to about 40 inches. The meat is somewhat dark and more pronounced in flavor than albacore, but may be cooked in some of the same ways (see pages 37-40); poaching, however, is not recommended. It is wise to cut out the very dark lines of flesh on either side of the fish before cooking. Two bonito recipes are on page 54.

SHEEPSHEAD

This is a particularly ugly looking fish, averaging about 4 to 15 pounds, with large, canine-like teeth and a fatty hump on the forehead. The males are red and black, and the females are uniformly dull red; both have white chins.

The flesh of this fish is firm, white, and mild in flavor. If you catch a sheepshead, fillet it and use the mild, white fillets as you would those of lingcod, halibut, or rockfish (see pages 20-27).

KELP BASS AND SAND BASS

These two bass belong to the same family as the giant sea bass (a market fish in Southern California), but they are much smaller. Their size averages from 10 to 20 inches, and they are caught in Southern California waters. Like the giant sea bass, their meat is lean, white, and mild in flavor.

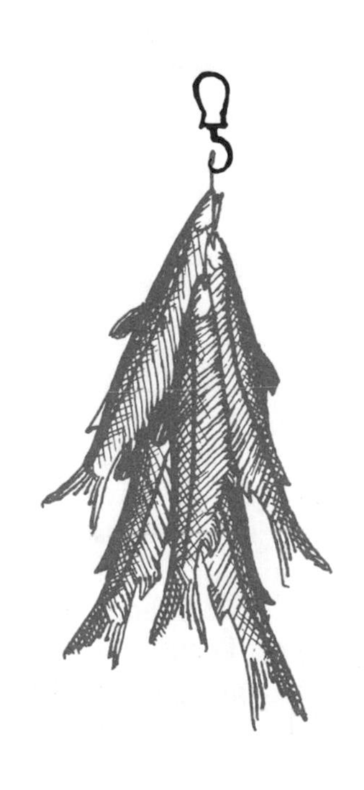

The larger fish may be cut into two whole fillets and cooked in any of the ways you might cook other lean white fish fillets (see pages 20-27). Smaller fish may be scaled and pan-dressed, then butter-sautéed as you would trout (see page 5). One recipe for these bass is included in this chapter.

STRIPED BASS

As with the kelp bass and sand bass, the striped bass is from the same fish family as the giant sea bass. It was introduced into the San Francisco area from the Atlantic Coast in 1879 and 1882, and now ranges from Coos Bay in Oregon to Southern California. Some are caught the year around in the Delta area of California.

Stripers are lean, white, and mild in flavor and considered especially good eating fish. The best way to prepare them for cooking is to fillet them and then skin the fillets (see pages 53-54). Use one of the special recipes for striped bass in this chapter, or cook the fillets as you would other lean white mild fish (see pages 20-27).

HOW TO PREPARE THE CATCH FOR COOKING

The wet sack of freshly caught fish brought home from a successful fishing jaunt requires some preparation before the catch is ready to be cooked. The questions of what to do and how to do it may baffle the inexperienced, but if you take the jobs step-by-step, it isn't difficult to clean, trim, and cut the fish into shape for cooking.

CLEANING

It is extremely important to the taste and texture of fish that it be cleaned (or drawn) as soon as possible after it is caught. Some fishermen prefer to clean each fish immediately after they catch it. On party fishing boats, a deck hand often cleans fish on the boat for a small charge. To clean fish yourself, simply cut the entire length of the belly and remove the entrails.

SCALING

This may be done either before or after the fish is cleaned; however, there's no need to scale a fish if you plan to skin it. When scaling, use a sharp kitchen knife or fisherman's scaler. Rinse the fish in cold water; then lay it on the table and, with one hand, hold the fish firmly by the head. Position the knife almost vertically and draw it from tail to head, scraping off the scales as you go. You can eliminate fiying scales by holding the fish under running water.

TRIMMING

If you plan to cook the whole fish, you may wish to leave the head and tail on, but you will want to remove the fins. Head, tail, and fins should be trimmed off before cutting steaks.

1) First cut around the pelvic fins and remove.

2) Next, cut off the head and pectoral fins by cutting above the collar bone. (If the backbone is large, cut down to it on each side of the fish; then snap the bone by bending it over the edge of the cutting board, or saw through the bone with a coping saw.)

3) Cut off the tail.

4) Remove the dorsal fin by cutting the flesh along both sides of the fin; then give a quick pull forward toward the head of the fish to remove the fin with the root bones attached.

5) Remove any other fins in the same way. Wash the fish in cold running water. The fish is now dressed or pan-dressed, depending on its size.

SKINNING

Some fish which are to be cooked whole are best if skinned in addition to being trimmed; examples are pan-dressed surfperch or dressed rockfish.

To skin a trimmed fish, work carefully with a sharp knife and separate a small portion of skin from the flesh at the head end of one side of the fish. Holding the head end of fish down with one hand, grasp the free portion of skin with the other hand and pull carefully back toward the tail. All the skin should come free from one side of the fish; repeat the process for the other side.

HOW TO PREPARE THE CATCH FOR COOKING

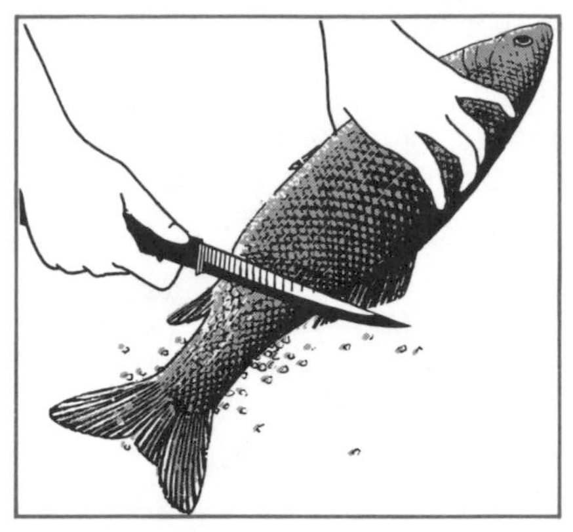

Scaling: Hold wet fish firmly by head; position knife almost vertically and draw from tail to head.

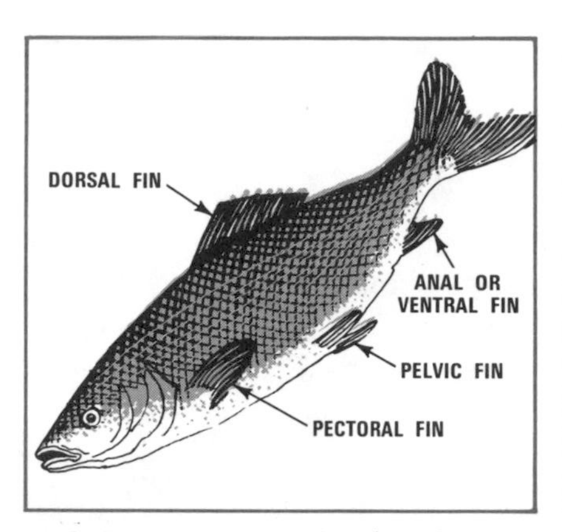

Fish fins: Cut around pelvic fins; remove them after cutting length of fish belly to remove entrails.

Trimming: Cut above collar bone to trim head, pectoral fins; if backbone is large, cut down to it, snap.

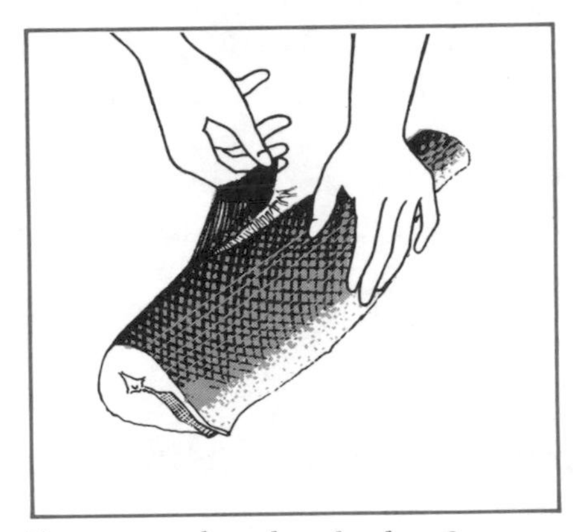

To remove dorsal and other fins, cut flesh on both sides; pull fin with root bones toward head of fish.

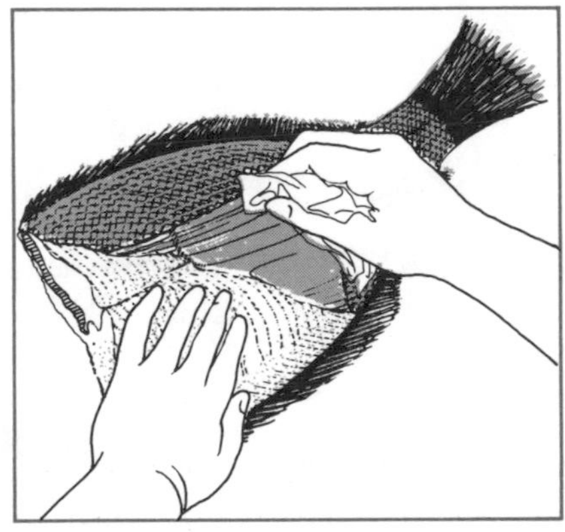

Skinning: Separate small portion of skin at head end of fish; grasp skin with cloth, pull toward tail.

Cutting steaks: Make steaks of preferred thickness by cutting across trimmed fish through backbone.

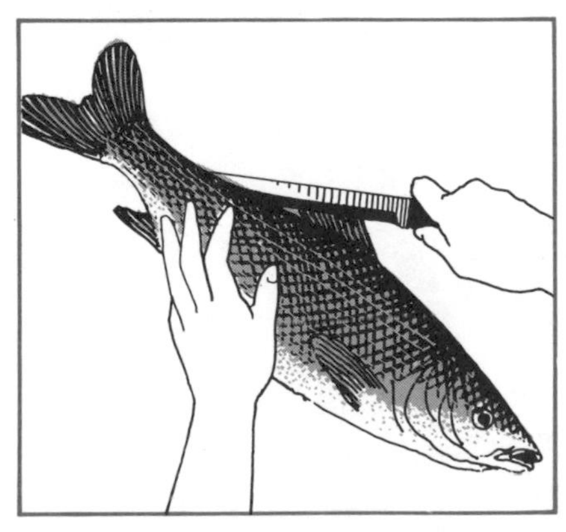

Filleting: With sharp knife, cut through flesh along the back from tail to just behind head of fish.

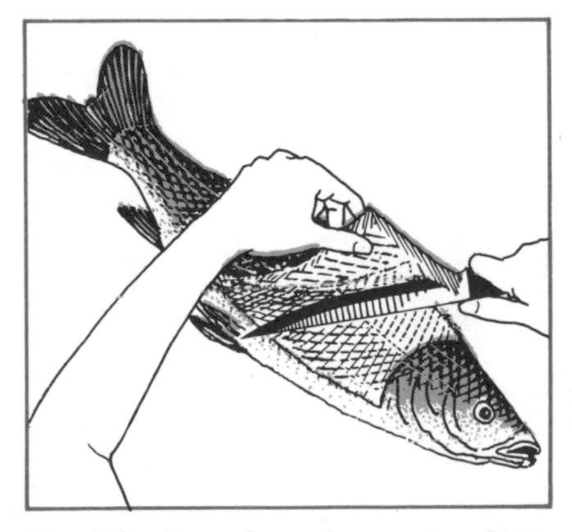

Cut fillet from bone by turning knife flat and running along the backbone and over the rib bones.

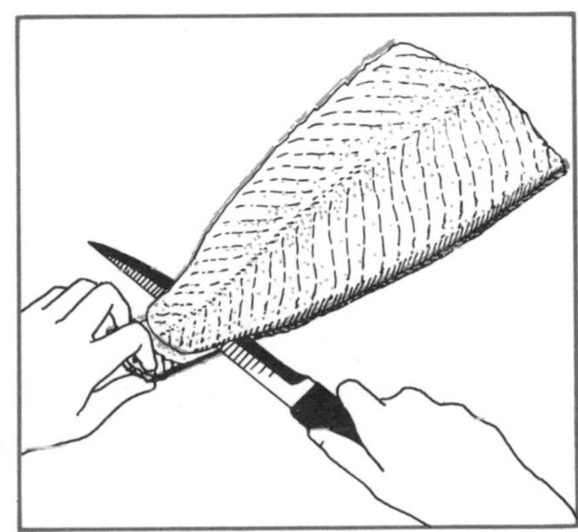

Skinning fillets: Cut down to skin at tail end of fillet; cut flesh from skin by pushing knife toward head.

CUTTING STEAKS

To make steaks of the thickness you prefer for cooking, simply cut across the trimmed fish, through the backbone.

FILLETING

Start with the whole, untrimmed fish; it should be scaled if you plan to leave the skin on the fillet.

1) With a sharp knife, cut through the flesh along the back from the tail to just behind the head of the fish.

2) Then cut down to the backbone, just above the collarbone.

3) Turn the knife flat and cut the flesh from the bone, allowing the knife to run along the backbone and over the rib bones.

4) Lift off the entire side of the fish in one piece; this is called a whole or single fillet.

5) Turn the fish over and repeat this procedure to remove the fillet from the other side.

SKINNING FILLETS

If you wish to skin a fillet, lay it flat on a cutting board with the skin side down. Hold the tail end with your fingers; using a sharp knife, cut through the flesh to the skin, about ½ inch from the tail end of the fillet. Flatten the knife on the skin and cut the flesh away from the skin by pushing the knife toward the head end while firmly holding the free end of the skin.

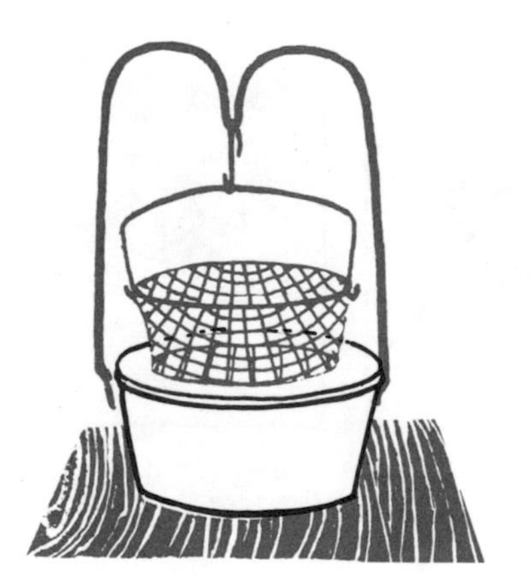

Braised Bonito

Cut thick steaks of bonito as directed for cutting albacore steaks on page 37; then remove the dark line of meat on either side of the fish.

6 bonito steaks (each 1 inch thick)
3 tablespoons butter
3 tablespoons salad oil
Salt and pepper to taste
1 medium-sized onion, sliced
2 medium-sized tomatoes, sliced
¼ cup dry white wine
¼ cup Espagnole sauce or canned beef gravy
¼ cup sliced cooked mushrooms (optional)

Brown the bonito steaks lightly on both sides in the butter and salad oil in a large frying pan. Sprinkle with salt and pepper to taste. Over them arrange the onion and tomato slices. Pour over fish the white wine mixed with the Espagnole sauce or canned beef gravy. Cover and simmer for 15 minutes. Remove fish to a hot serving platter; keep warm in the oven. Simmer the sauce a few minutes longer; then add the mushrooms, if desired. Pour the sauce over the fish. Makes 6 servings.

Stuffed Bonito with Tomatoes

Here you stuff a small whole bonito with a simple dressing and bake it in a flavorful tomato sauce.

1 small bonito (3 to 5 lbs., whole weight)
½ cup finely minced onion
¼ cup butter
1 cup toasted fresh bread crumbs
½ teaspoon salt
½ teaspoon thyme
2 medium-sized onions, sliced
3 tablespoons butter
1 large can (1 lb., 12 oz.) tomatoes
1½ teaspoons salt
½ teaspoon pepper
Pinch thyme

Clean and dress the bonito as directed on pages 52-53. Fill the cavity with a simple bread stuffing made as follows: Sauté the ½ cup finely minced onion in the ¼ cup butter; mix with toasted bread crumbs and season with the ½ teaspoon salt and ½ teaspoon thyme. Sew or skewer the fish together and place in a greased shallow baking dish.

Sauté the sliced onions in the 3 tablespoons butter; add tomatoes, the 1½ teaspoons salt, pepper, and pinch of thyme. Cook, stirring, until thickened. Pour this sauce over the fish and bake, uncovered, in a hot oven (400°) for 25 minutes, or until the fish tests done. Makes 4 to 6 servings.

Fish Ragout

Tomato-based stew is a good flavor background for a variety of fish and provides a way to use some of the sportfisherman's catch.

1 medium-sized onion, chopped
1 clove garlic, minced or mashed
3 tablespoons olive oil or salad oil
1 large can (1 lb., 12 oz.) tomatoes
1 can (6 oz.) tomato paste
½ cup finely minced parsley
1 teaspoon basil
¾ teaspoon oregano
½ bay leaf
1½ cups dry white wine (or 1¼ cups water and ¼ cup lemon juice)
3 stalks celery, cut in ½-inch slices
1 teaspoon salt
¼ teaspoon pepper
3 to 4 pounds fish (almost any fish can be used, and assorted varieties are fine — rockfish, mackerel, bonito, barracuda, perch)

In a large heavy pan, such as a Dutch oven, sauté the onion and garlic in the heated oil until tender, about 5 minutes. Add the tomatoes (break up large pieces), tomato paste, parsley, basil, oregano, bay leaf, wine, celery, salt, and pepper. Cover and simmer gently for about 1 hour. Meanwhile, cut the fish into large chunks, removing bones. Add to the pan and simmer about 15 minutes, or until fish is tender. Remove bay leaf before serving. Serve in large soup plates. Makes about 8 servings.

Butter-Sautéed Bass

Try this slight variation of the basic method of butter-sautéing for excellent results with small Pacific Coast bass, kelp bass, or sand bass fillets.

Fillet the bass as directed on pages 53-54; they need not be skinned. Dip bass fillets in mixture of beaten egg, melted butter, and salt and pepper (with each egg, use 1 tablespoon melted butter, about ¼ teaspoon salt, and about ¼ teaspoon pepper). Then roll in fine cracker crumbs to coat lightly on both sides. Heat a mixture of half salad oil and half butter to make about a ⅛-inch layer in a heavy frying pan. Brown fillets over medium-high heat for about 2 minutes on the flesh side; turn carefully and fry 4 to 5 minutes on the skin side. Serve with tartare sauce, if you wish (see page 10).

Barbecued Striped Bass

Fillet and skin a striped bass weighing 7 to 8 pounds (see filleting directions on pages 53-54). Chill fillets for 30 minutes. Place in a single layer in a hinged broiler about 6 inches from heat and cook over hot coals, turning occasionally and basting frequently with barbecue sauce (recipe follows). Cook just until flesh flakes easily when tested with a fork, about 20 minutes total cooking time. Serve with remaining sauce. Makes 8 to 10 servings.

BARBECUE SAUCE:

¾ cup chopped onions
½ cup salad oil
¾ cup tomato catsup
¾ cup water
⅓ cup lemon juice
3 tablespoons sugar
3 tablespoons Worcestershire
2 tablespoons prepared mustard
2 teaspoons salt
½ teaspoon pepper

Cook onions in salad oil until soft. Add tomato catsup, water, lemon juice, sugar, Worcestershire, prepared mustard, salt, and pepper; let simmer 15 minutes.

Stuffed Striped Bass with Tomato Sauce

You start with skinned fillets to make this exceptional bass recipe.

1 whole striped bass (4 to 5 lbs.)
¼ cup chopped fresh parsley
¾ cup finely chopped onion
¾ cup finely chopped celery
About 1½ teaspoons salt
½ teaspoon pepper
3 slices bacon, uncooked
3 thin lemon slices
1 can (8 oz.) tomato sauce

Fillet and skin the bass as directed on pages 53-54. Place one fillet in a greased shallow baking dish. Arrange on it this stuffing: Mix parsley, onion, and celery; season with salt and pepper. Top stuffing with the second fillet. Arrange uncooked bacon and lemon slices over the fish. Bake, uncovered, in a moderate oven (350°) for about 25 minutes. Pour tomato sauce over fish; return to oven and bake about 5 minutes more, or until fish flakes easily with a fork. Makes 6 to 8 servings.

Baked Bass with Cheese Crumb Topping

1 whole striped bass (4 to 5 lbs.)
2 tablespoons olive oil or salad oil
About 1 tablespoon salt
½ teaspoon pepper
½ cup soft bread crumbs
2 tablespoons grated Parmesan cheese
½ cup chopped parsley
1 can (8 oz.) tomato sauce
1 sauce can water

Fillet the bass as directed on pages 53-54, but leave the skin on fillets. Place the 2 fillets, skin side down, in a baking pan. Sprinkle over fish the olive oil or salad oil; sprinkle with salt and pepper. Set into a moderate oven (350°) for 5 minutes. Meanwhile combine bread crumbs with Parmesan cheese and parsley. Sprinkle crumb mixture over fish and bake about 15 minutes longer. Combine tomato sauce with water and pour over fish; continue baking 10 to 15 minutes, or until the fish flakes easily with a fork. Makes 6 to 8 servings.

Striped Bass Cioppino

In a large saucepan, brown 2 medium-sized onions, sliced, in 2 tablespoons olive oil or salad oil. Add 3 cans (8 oz. each) tomato sauce and an equal amount (3 cans) water; simmer 8 to 10 minutes. Stir in 2 medium-sized potatoes, cut in about ¾-inch cubes; 1 green pepper, thinly sliced; 1 teaspoon salt; and ½ teaspoon pepper. Add 4 pounds skinned striped bass fillets (from a 5 to 6-lb. whole fish), cut in strips 1½ inches wide (see pages 53-54 for filleting instructions). Cover and simmer gently until potatoes are cooked; takes 15 to 20 minutes. Serve in bowls. Makes 6 to 8 servings.

Striped Bass with Carrot Stuffing

1 whole striped bass (about 4 lbs.)
3 medium-sized carrots, coarsely shredded
⅓ cup finely chopped celery
¼ cup chopped parsley
1 can (10¼ oz.) condensed cream of mushroom soup
¾ cup dry white wine

Fillet and skin the bass (see pages 53-54). Place one fillet in the bottom of a greased shallow baking dish. Spread carrots on top of fillet. Top with celery and parsley. Arrange the second fillet over the vegetables. Pour the mushroom soup over the fish. Cover the pan (use foil if it doesn't have a lid). Bake in a hot oven (400°) for 15 minutes. Remove the cover and bake 15 minutes longer, or until fish flakes when tested with a fork. Pour the white wine over the fish; mix gently with the mushroom sauce. Serve immediately. Makes about 6 servings.

SHRIMP

Fresh, Frozen, Canned

The shrimp we buy are actually only the tail sections of the shellfish. Since there is practically no meat on the head sections, these are removed and discarded either on the fishing boats before they are landed or in the packing and canning plants. The term "shrimp" refers to these heads-off shrimp.

Shrimp are available raw or cooked, shelled or unshelled, and you can buy them fresh, frozen, or canned. For the most part, they can be used interchangeably in recipes. You may find it useful to know that 2 pounds of raw shrimp in shells will yield about 1 pound cooked, shelled, and deveined meat. When you purchase cooked shrimp in the shells, you will need about 1¼ pounds to yield 1 pound of shelled meat.

Customarily, shrimp are sold according to the size or count in a pound. The plentiful tiny ocean shrimp, which are always sold shelled and cooked, come 150 to 180 to a pound. Other shrimp sizes will vary from small (45 to 65 count), medium (30 count average), to large (6 to 15 count); these are sold raw, cooked, shelled, or unshelled.

Biologically speaking, all sizes of shrimp belong to the same group of Crustacea. The word "prawn" is used in some areas to designate the largest sized shrimp. Raw shrimp are often called "green shrimp" in retail stores.

HOW TO DEVEIN RAW SHRIMP

To give shrimp the most attractive appearance, devein them with a skewer before they are cooked; then they will not have a cut down the center of the back. You can devein raw shrimp by this method either before or after they have been shucked:

Insert a slender sharp skewer or pick beneath the vein in about the middle of the back and carefully pull the vein out. If the vein should break, insert the skewer somewhere along the remaining length of vein and repeat the process in several places if necessary.

HOW TO COOK SHRIMP

The general rules for fish cookery apply to shrimp: Don't overcook, and don't use too high a temperature. Long cooking or high heat will toughen and shrink the shrimp. Cook them before or after shelling. If you plan to use the cooking liquid, cook the shrimp in their shells to give extra shrimp flavor to the liquid.

For 1 to 2 pounds of shelled or unshelled raw shrimp, bring to a boil 1 quart water with 2 tablespoons salt (or 1 quart basic poaching liquid given on page 7). Add the shrimp and simmer, but do not boil, for 5 to 8 minutes, depending on the size of the shrimp; drain and chill. If the shrimp have not been deveined before cooking, make a shallow cut lengthwise down the backs and rinse out the sand veins.

Shrimp Cocktail Sauce

Here is a sauce for shrimp, lobster, or other shellfish that is neither too red nor too sweet.

Purée 1 very small clove garlic with a garlic press. Combine with ½ cup commercial sour cream, ¼ cup canned tomato sauce, 1 tablespoon Cognac (optional), 1 tablespoon anchovy paste, 1 tablespoon lemon juice, a dash of liquid hot-pepper seasoning, and 1 teaspoon minced fresh dill or ½ teaspoon dill weed. Mix well and chill.

Iced Shrimp in Dill Marinade

Serve iced shrimp as an appetizer or for a first course with rye wafer bread.

Devein 2 pounds large raw shrimp or prawns (about 40 to a pound). Cook as directed on page 57. Drain; reserve ¾ cup of the cooking liquid. Shell shrimp and pour marinade over them. To make marinade, mix ¾ cup cooking liquid with ½ cup lemon juice, 1 teaspoon dill weed, 3 tablespoons minced onion, 2 teaspoons sugar, 1 teaspoon salt, and ¼ teaspoon ground allspice. Cover and chill for at least 4 hours (or overnight). Serve shrimp from a well chilled or iced container. Garnish, if you like, with fresh dill or parsley sprigs. Serve with lemon wedges and rye wafer bread. Makes 6 servings.

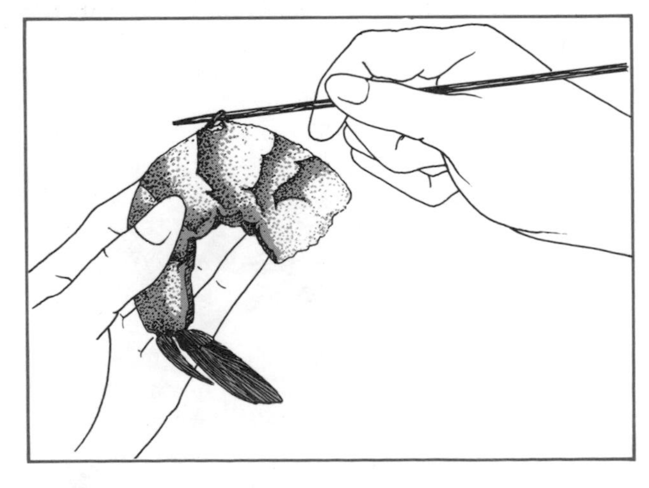

Deveining raw shrimp: Insert skewer beneath vein in middle of back, carefully pull out; repeat as needed.

Butterflied Shrimp Appetizer

Butterflied shrimp appetizers are skewered and barbecued over hot coals. Squeeze a little lime juice over them just before serving.

Remove shells, tails, and veins from 1 pound large or medium-sized raw shrimp. Slit each shrimp down back side, cutting almost all the way through so it will lay out flat (take care not to cut entirely in half). Dip shrimp into 1 egg slightly beaten with ¼ teaspoon salt and ¼ teaspoon pepper, then into fine dry bread crumbs to coat each side (you'll need about ½ cup of the crumbs). Thread each shrimp on a single, long, thin bamboo skewer. Insert point of skewer at tail of shrimp and impale its full length so that the point of skewer just shows at head end of shrimp. Refrigerate until ready to cook. Cook over hot coals; baste occasionally with a mixture of ½ cup melted butter and ¼ cup lime or lemon juice. Serve with lime wedges to squeeze over shrimp. Makes about 16 large or 25 medium appetizers.

Hot Shrimp with Dill Butter

Try hot shrimp with dill butter for a very informal, out-of-doors party. Have a big pot of boiling salted water on the charcoal grill, camp stove, or electric plate; then provide plenty of large raw shrimp, their shells still on, but deveined as directed on pages 57-58.

Let each guest boil his own shrimp, taking them out with tongs or slotted spoons which you have provided. You will also need plenty of hot towels (fingertip terry towels, wrung out in hot water) and dill butter (recipe follows). The shrimp are done when they turn pink and should be shelled as soon as they are cool enough to handle; don't let them get too cool.

DILL BUTTER:

Melt butter, allowing ⅛ pound (¼ cup) for each person; add 1 teaspoon minced fresh dill or dill weed and a few drops lemon juice for each person to be served.

Fried Shrimp Balls

These simple to make hot appetizers originated in Southeast Asia.

2 pounds raw shrimp, shelled and deveined
1 slice bacon, minced
1 egg, slightly beaten
1 tablespoon cornstarch
1 can (5 oz.) water chestnuts, drained and chopped
3 tablespoons chopped green onions
1 teaspoon salt
¼ teaspoon ground ginger
¼ teaspoon pepper
2 cups salad oil
Prepared seafood cocktail sauce

Dice shrimp and combine in a bowl with bacon, egg, cornstarch, water chestnuts, green onions, salt, ground ginger, and pepper. (This much you can prepare ahead and refrigerate.) Heat salad oil in a large frying pan to about 350°. Drop shrimp mixture (about ½ teaspoon at a time) into hot oil. Cook, turning, until shrimp balls turn pink, about 2 minutes. Remove from oil with slotted spoon; drain on paper towels. Serve hot with a prepared seafood cocktail sauce. Makes about 90 appetizers.

Shrimp Toast Canapés

Quickly broil shrimp toast canapés just before you serve them.

1 pound raw shrimp
1 green onion, including part of green top
4 canned water chestnuts
½ teaspoon salt
¼ teaspoon garlic salt
⅛ teaspoon pepper
1½ teaspoons lemon juice
1 egg white
12 thin slices white sandwich bread, crusts removed
About 2 tablespoons melted butter

Shell and devein the raw shrimp. Chop shrimp, onion, and water chestnuts into very fine pieces. Put into a bowl with the salt, garlic salt, pepper, and lemon juice. Mix until well blended. Add unbeaten egg white, mixing it in well. Put bread slices under the broiler until toasted on one side. Turn over and spread untoasted side with the shrimp mixture. This much can be done several hours ahead and the appetizers covered with clear plastic film or foil.

Just before serving, brush the top of each sandwich with melted butter and broil until the shrimp topping turns pink. Cut into quarters and serve hot. Makes about 4 dozen square canapés.

Hot Prawn and Grapefruit Cocktail

This hot (in temperature) seafood cocktail is a novel departure, and a tasty one.

½ cup catsup
¼ cup chile sauce
¼ cup grapefruit juice
2 tablespoons lemon juice
1 tablespoon thinly sliced green onions with tops
¾ teaspoon salt
1 teaspoon prepared horseradish
1½ teaspoons Worcestershire
2 or 3 drops liquid hot-pepper seasoning
1 tablespoon butter
1½ pounds large raw shrimp (about 40 to the pound), shelled and deveined
1½ cups grapefruit segments, all white membrane removed
Sliced green onions

In a saucepan combine catsup, chile sauce, grapefruit juice, lemon juice, onions, salt, horseradish, Worcestershire, liquid hot-pepper seasoning, and butter. Bring to simmering; add shrimp and cook, stirring, for about 6 minutes. Add grapefruit and heat through. Spoon hot mixture into small shallow bowls and scatter with the extra sliced green onions. Makes 8 servings.

Tomato Slices with Shrimp Topping

When the day calls for a light lunch, cut thick slices from large beefsteak tomatoes and serve them generously topped with seafood.

- *1 can (about 4½ oz.) shrimp, rinsed and drained, or about 1 cup cooked and deveined small shrimp*
- *2 hard-cooked eggs, chopped*
- *1½ cups shredded raw carrots*
- *1 tablespoon minced green onion*
- *½ cup mayonnaise*
- *2 tablespoons lemon juice*
- *½ teaspoon prepared mustard*
- *Salt and pepper to taste*
- *2 or 3 large tomatoes or 4 to 6 medium-sized tomatoes*
- *Lettuce*

Combine the drained or cooked shrimp with the eggs, carrots, and green onion. In a small bowl blend together the mayonnaise, lemon juice, and mustard; add to the shrimp mixture and stir until blended. Taste, then add salt and pepper, if needed. Peel the tomatoes, cut off ends (save for salad another day); slice each tomato into about 2 thick slices. Arrange one or two of the slices on a bed of lettuce on each serving plate. Divide the shrimp mixture equally, mounding it on top of the tomato on each plate. You could garnish each salad with a few additional shrimp, or hard-cook an extra egg and use to garnish salads. Makes 4 to 6 servings.

Eggs Fried with Shrimp and Dill

You can cook and serve this dish right at the table using an electric frying pan or chafing dish. Have the butter, salt, and dill in the cooking pan when you bring it to the table. The cleaned shrimp can be in one bowl, the whole eggs in another, and the cream in a small pitcher. A small salad dressing bottle works as a miniature decanter for sherry. You will need a wide spatula to serve the fried eggs and prawns.

- *2 tablespoons butter*
- *½ teaspoon salt*
- *¼ teaspoon dill weed*
- *1 pound raw prawns or large shrimp (40 to the pound), shelled and deveined*
- *4 eggs*
- *2 tablespoons heavy cream*
- *Sherry (about 2 teaspoons)*

Melt butter with salt and dill in a wide pan over direct heat. Add the shrimp and cook, stirring just until they begin to turn pink, about 2 minutes. Make 4 spaces among the prawns and break an egg into each spot. Pour cream over eggs; cover pan and cook until eggs are set to suit your taste. Pass sherry and let each person drizzle about ½ teaspoon over each egg. Makes 2 or 4 servings.

Dilled Shrimp-and-Cheese Rolls

Garnish hot shrimp and cheese sandwiches with a skewered shrimp curled around a stuffed olive.

- *1½ pounds medium-sized raw shrimp*
- *¾ cup cubed Tybo, Gruyère, or Samsoe cheese*
- *¼ cup sliced green onions, including part of tops*
- *½ teaspoon dill weed*
- *¾ teaspoon salt*
- *⅓ cup mayonnaise*
- *1½ teaspoons white wine vinegar*
- *6 sesame seed sandwich rolls, split and buttered*
- *6 stuffed olives for garnish*

Cook, shell, and devein shrimp; chop coarsely, reserving 6 whole shrimp for garnish (you should have about 2½ cups chopped shrimp). Stir in cheese, green onions, dill weed, salt, mayonnaise, and vinegar until shrimp is well coated. Spread sandwich rolls with shrimp mixture; wrap individually in foil.

Bake in a moderate oven (350°) for about 20 minutes or until cheese begins to melt. Unwrap and serve garnished with olives and reserved shrimp on wooden picks. Makes 6 sandwiches.

Dilled shrimp-and-cheese rolls are wrapped in foil to bake.They can be prepared and refrigerated for several hours, then baked just before mealtime. A skewered shrimp makes an attractive garnish.

Shrimp and Potato Salad

Pastel tints of pink and green make shrimp and potato salad an attractive choice for a luncheon. All you need to complete lunch are bread and butter sandwiches (use pumpernickel or rye bread if you wish), iced tea or coffee, and a dessert.

Devein 2 pounds (30 to 40 to the pound) raw shrimp without shelling (see directions on pages 57-58). Drop shrimp into boiling salted water to cover, and cook for 4 minutes, or until bright pink. Drain and let stand until cool enough to touch; shell, chop into large pieces, and set aside.

Peel and dice enough boiling potatoes to make 4 cups. Cook in boiling salted water to cover, until potatoes are tender, about 8 minutes. Drain and let cool slightly.

Meanwhile, combine in a blender ½ cup chopped parsley, ¼ cup chopped chives (fresh, frozen, or freeze-dried), 5 anchovies rolled around capers (about half of a 2-oz. can), and 1½ cups mayonnaise. Whirl smooth (or very finely mince parsley, chives, and anchovies, and blend with mayonnaise).

Mix together the chopped shrimp, cooked potatoes, and mayonnaise mixture. Mold the salad by turning it into a deep pan (about 2-quart size) with smooth sides and flat bottom, or simply mound salad on a serving tray or in a bowl; chill. Turn salad out of mold (smooth with a knife) and garnish with about 1 cup tiny cooked shelled shrimp and cucumber slices. To make a crown for the molded salad, stand shrimp close together, vertically, around top edge. Makes 6 to 8 servings.

Curried Shrimp

Curried shrimp keeps well in a chafing dish for one to two hours.

1 pound medium-sized raw shrimp
Boiling, salted water
¼ cup (⅛ lb.) butter or margarine
⅓ cup chopped onion
¼ cup chopped green pepper
1 clove garlic, minced or mashed
1 teaspoon curry powder
3 tablespoons flour
2 cups half-and-half (half milk, half cream) or light cream
1 tablespoon lemon juice
½ teaspoon salt
⅛ teaspoon ground ginger
⅛ teaspoon pepper
⅛ teaspoon chile powder
Hot cooked rice

Cook shrimp in boiling, salted water until they turn pink, about 5 minutes. Drain and cool; then shell, devein, and set aside. In a pan or chafing dish over direct heat, melt the butter; add onion and green pepper and sauté until tender, about 5 minutes. Add garlic, curry powder, and flour; heat and stir until bubbly. Remove from heat and stir in the cream, lemon juice, salt, and remaining seasonings. Cook, stirring, until thickened. Add the shrimp and heat through. Taste, and add more curry or salt, if needed. Set over hot water to keep warm (it keeps well up to about 2 hours). Serve over hot, cooked rice. Makes about 6 servings.

Fan-Tail Shrimp

This method of cutting and frying shrimp results in an interesting fan-tail shape.

1 pound large raw shrimp or prawns
2 eggs
1½ teaspoons sugar
½ teaspoon salt
¼ teaspoon pepper
¼ cup flour
Salad oil or shortening for frying

Wash, shell and devein shrimp, leaving the tails on. Cut a slit starting about ½ inch from head end and running to within about ½ inch of tail. Pull tail through slit to make a butterflied, fan-tailed shape. Beat eggs slightly and add sugar, salt, pepper, and flour, and mix well. Dip shrimp in egg mixture; drain briefly; then cook in deep fat (heated to 375°) until golden brown, about 3 minutes on each side. Serve hot. Makes 4 servings.

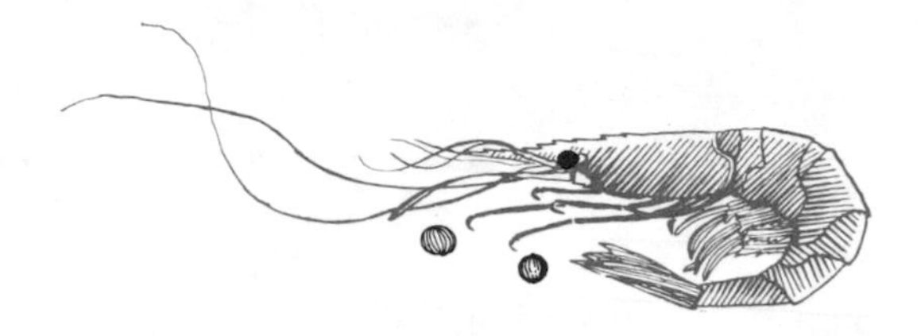

Paella Valenciana

There are many versions of paella; they vary from region to region in Spain. This version, typical of Valencia, makes prominent use of large shrimp.

⅓ cup olive oil, or 2½ tablespoons olive oil and 2½ tablespoons butter
1 pound lean pork spareribs, cut apart
¾ pound (12 oz.) chorizos (Spanish or Mexican sausage)
2 cloves garlic, minced or mashed
3 large tomatoes, peeled and cut into wedges
6 cups water
2 teaspoons salt
¼ teaspoon pepper
1 to 2 dozen small clams in shells (or use mussels when in season)
1 to 1½ pounds large raw shrimp
2 cups long-grain rice
1 can (4 oz.) pimiento, sliced
1 cup fresh or frozen peas
¼ cup chopped parsley

Heat the olive oil in a large heavy pan; add the spareribs and brown well on all sides. Remove casings from chorizos; add to pan and brown. Add garlic, tomatoes, water, salt, and pepper. Simmer for 20 minutes. Meanwhile, scrub clams or mussels well to remove all sand and barnacles. Shell and remove sand vein from shrimp. Slowly add rice to simmering mixture; then add clams and shrimp. Cook slowly for about 20 minutes, stirring occasionally. Add pimientos, peas, and parsley, and cook about 10 minutes longer, or until the rice is tender. Serve immediately. Makes 6 to 8 servings.

Shrimp Tetrazzini

Among the favorite seafood Tetrazzini recipes is this spice-filled one made with cooked shrimp.

½ cup (¼ lb.) butter or margarine
1 cup thinly sliced green onions, including some of the tops
5 tablespoons flour
2½ cups chicken broth, canned or freshly made
½ cup clam juice
½ cup dry white wine
½ cup heavy cream
½ teaspoon oregano
½ cup shredded Parmesan cheese
2 whole cloves garlic
½ pound mushrooms, sliced
Salted water
8 ounces noodles (spaghetti or vermicelli)
4 cups deveined, cooked, shelled shrimp
Salt

Melt ¼ cup of the butter in a pan, add onions, and cook, stirring, until soft. Mix in flour and gradually blend in chicken broth, clam juice, wine, cream, and oregano. Cook, stirring, for about 3 minutes after sauce begins to simmer. Stir in ¼ cup of the cheese. Set sauce aside.

Melt the remaining butter in another pan; add the garlic and mushrooms and cook quickly until lightly browned. Discard garlic.

Also bring to a boil a quantity of salted water; add the noodles and cook them until they are tender to bite, but not soft; then drain.

Combine sauce, mushrooms, noodles, shrimp (save a few shrimp for garnish if you like), and season with salt to taste. Pour into a large shallow casserole or individual casseroles. Top with shrimp and sprinkle with remaining cheese. Bake in a moderately hot oven (375°) until bubbling; allow 15 minutes for large casserole or 8 minutes for small ones. Broil top until lightly browned. Makes 6 to 8 servings.

Hawaiian Shrimp Curry

Coconut milk and cucumber add unique flavor and texture to shrimp curry. You can buy frozen coconut milk in pints in many supermarkets, or make it yourself using the following directions: Pour 2 cups scalded milk over 4 cups grated fresh coconut; leave 20 minutes. Strain through two thicknesses of cheesecloth; squeeze out all the liquid.

3 medium onions, chopped
2 tablespoons butter or margarine
5 tablespoons flour (7 tablespoons flour if homogenized milk is used)
1 tablespoon curry powder
1½ teaspoons salt
1½ teaspoons sugar
¼ teaspoon powdered ginger
1 bouillon cube in 1 cup boiling water
2 cups coconut milk (or homogenized milk)
2 pounds raw shrimp, shelled and deveined
2 cucumbers, peeled, in 2½-inch strips
1½ teaspoons onion juice
Hot cooked rice

Sauté onion in butter until golden; put aside. Make a paste of flour, curry powder, salt, sugar, ginger, and ½ cup of the bouillon. Combine this with the onion, remaining bouillon, coconut milk, and shrimp in a large saucepan. Cook over a low heat, stirring constantly, until thick (15 to 20 minutes). Drop cucumber strips into boiling water and cook for 2 minutes; drain immediately and add with onion juice to shrimp mixture. Serve over hot rice. Makes 6 to 8 servings.

Condiments: Prepare about ¾ cup *each* of the following: minced green pepper, chopped crisp bacon, salted peanuts, sieved cooked egg white (season with dash of monosodium glutamate and cayenne pepper), sieved cooked egg yolk, mango chutney, and flaked coconut.

LOBSTER

Spiny Pacific and Northeastern

Spiny lobsters that range along the West Coast from approximately San Luis Obispo County, California, into Mexico are of a different genus of Crustacea than the lobsters of the Northeastern American coast. Lacking the large anterior claws of the Northern lobsters, the spiny, or rock lobster, has all its meat concentrated in the tail.

Frozen lobster tails and whole lobsters, which are imported from various waters around the world, are all of the spiny lobster type. These lobsters vary somewhat in tenderness, and it is generally agreed that those from Mexican and Australian-Tasmanian waters have the juiciest and tenderest meat. Frozen langostinas in our markets are a miniature variety of lobster, usually about as large as a medium-sized shrimp.

The firm white meat of lobster is tender and delicately sweet in flavor if properly cooked. To appreciate lobster meat at its best, lobster should be alive until you cook it. Live Pacific spiny lobsters are often available in waterfront markets of California, especially in Southern California; inland fish markets can usually special order them if given a few days' notice. Live Northern lobsters are available in many specialty fish markets on the West Coast.

Most lobster tails are frozen uncooked, so they need to be cooked before you eat them. The whole lobsters are usually cooked before freezing and shipping (you can tell by the bright red or orange color), so you need only thaw the meat for cold dishes, or heat it through for hot dishes. Frozen langostinas in our markets are usually shelled and cooked, ready to eat when thawed; use them in salads or in other ways you would use cooked or canned lobster meat.

HOW TO PREPARE LIVE LOBSTERS

If you purchase live lobsters, either spiny or Northern, there is a choice of ways to prepare them: They may be boiled and then cleaned to serve hot with melted butter, or you can serve them chilled with mayonnaise or another cold fish sauce. Live Northern lobsters may be killed, cleaned, split, and then broiled or baked; although this method is not for the squeamish, it results in the most succulent and tender broiled lobster. Spiny lobsters are much easier to handle if they are first boiled, then cleaned and split for broiling or baking (you may prefer this method also for Northern lobster); but care must then be taken only to reheat the meat, not further cook it.

TO BOIL LIVE LOBSTERS:

In a large pan, bring to boiling enough water to generously cover the lobsters; add about 1 tablespoon salt for each quart water. Grasp lobster from behind large front claws or front legs (you may wish to wear gloves when handling spiny lobsters

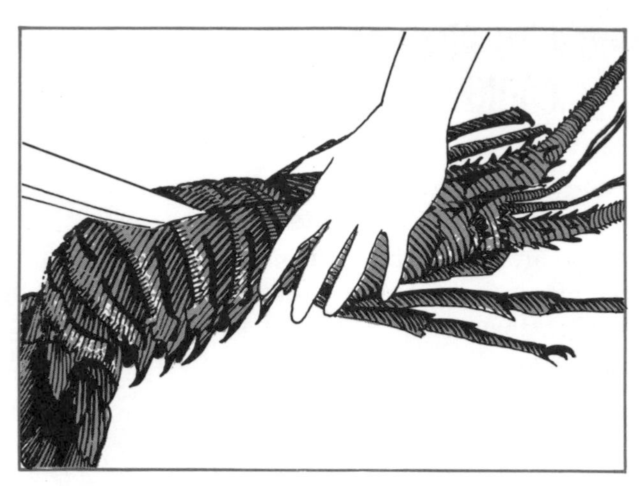

To clean a spiny lobster, use a sharp, heavy knife and split lobster end to end through the shell.

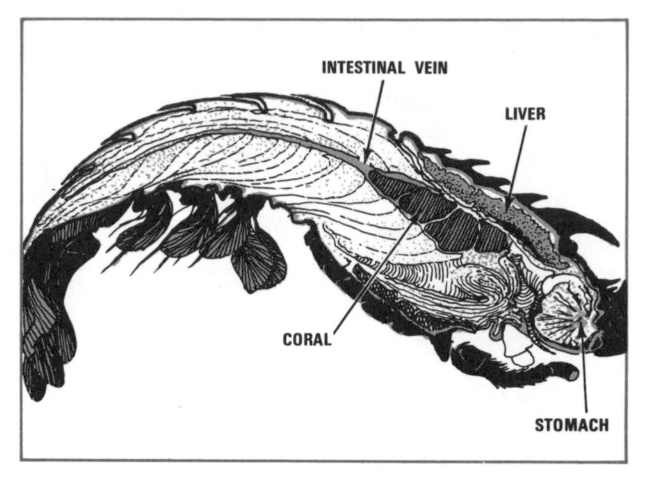

Remove the small sac (stomach) just behind head; pull out intestinal vein. Save roe and yellow liver.

to protect your hands from the sharp spines). Plunge lobsters headfirst into the boiling water; bring water back to simmering; then cover and simmer about 7 minutes for a 1-pound lobster, or about 10 minutes for 2-pound ones. Remove and plunge into cold water; rinse and drain.

TO CLEAN COOKED LOBSTER:

With a sharp knife, split lobster end to end through the shell. Remove the small sac (stomach), which lies just behind the head, and pull out the intestinal vein, which runs down to the end of the tail. Do not discard the coral colored roe (if any) or the yellow liver. Twist off and discard spiny lobster legs. Crack the claws of Northern lobsters. If you wish to remove all the meat from a spiny lobster at once, grasp tail and body and bend the shell backward at the joint until it breaks. Directions for broiling or barbecuing a cooked lobster are on page 66.

TO SERVE COOKED LOBSTER:

Warm, freshly cooked lobsters are delicious served simply with melted butter. If you have lobster with roe, you can remove the roe when cleaning and beat it into soft butter (use about ¼ to ½ cup butter with the roe of each lobster); serve in place of melted butter. With chilled, cooked lobster, you can serve plain mayonnaise, lemon mayonnaise, or green mayonnaise (recipes on page 72).

To eat, use a lobster or nut cracker to crack the big claw shells of Northern lobster. Break off the small legs of either type of lobster and suck out the morsels of meat and juices inside. Use a fork and start at the tip end to lift out the tail meat in one piece; then cut it with a knife and fork into bite-sized pieces.

TO BROIL UNCOOKED NORTHERN LOBSTER:

First kill the lobster; this can be done instantly by holding the lobster on its back and inserting the tip of a sharp knife between the tail section and the body shell, cutting to sever the spinal cord. Split the lobster lengthwise and remove the stomach and intestinal vein as described at left.

Place the split lobster on the broiler rack with meat sides up. Brush the meat generously with melted butter, or spread with whipped lemon butter (recipe on page 66). Place about 4 inches from the source of heat and broil for 10 to 12 minutes, until the meat is golden brown. Serve lobster immediately.

HOW TO PREPARE FROZEN LOBSTER TAILS

Lobster tails are usually frozen uncooked; to cook them, you may either boil or broil. An important point to remember is that they should be completely thawed before cooking.

TO BOIL LOBSTER TAILS:

Plunge the thawed tails into boiling water with about 1 tablespoon salt for each quart of water used. When the water resumes boiling, cover the pan and simmer about 5 minutes for 4-ounce tails; add 1 minute for each additional ounce. Remove and plunge into cold water; drain.

TO BROIL LOBSTER TAILS:

Use kitchen scissors to cut along the underside of the thawed lobster tail, clipping off the many fins along the outer edges. Peel back the soft undershell and discard. Bend the shell back, cracking some of the joints to prevent curling. Arrange on broiler pan, shell side up, and broil 5 inches from heat for 4 minutes. Turn over and spread meat with whipped lemon butter (recipe follows), and broil about 5 minutes longer. (If lobster tails are large, split them lengthwise into 2 servings each; arrange split tails, meat side up, on broiler pan; spread with whipped lemon butter and broil 4 inches from heat for about 5 minutes.) Serve immediately.

Whipped Lemon Butter:

Cream ⅓ cup butter until soft. Add 2 teaspoons minced parsley, dash of salt, and 2 tablespoons lemon juice; beat until fluffy. Makes 4 servings.

HOW TO PREPARE PRECOOKED LOBSTERS

When you buy whole lobsters that are bright red or orange in color, they have already been cooked; these are ready for use in salads and cold dishes, or may be reheated by broiling or barbecuing. If frozen, thaw completely before reheating; split and clean as directed on page 65, under "To Clean Cooked Lobster."

TO BROIL COOKED LOBSTER:

Spread each half of the split, cleaned lobster with melted butter or whipped lemon butter (recipe on this page); broil 4 to 5 inches from the source of heat for about 4 minutes, or just until the lobster is heated through.

TO BARBECUE COOKED LOBSTER:

Spread each half of the split, cleaned lobster with melted butter or whipped lemon butter (recipe on this page); wrap each half in foil and place, shell side down, on a grill over medium heat just until lobster is heated through; this will take about 15 minutes.

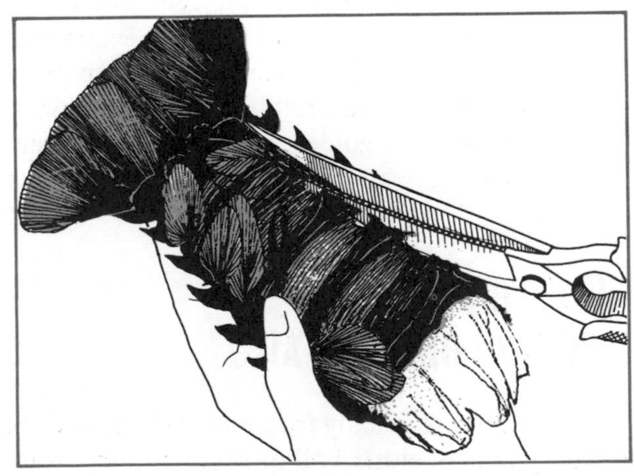

To prepare lobster tails, use scissors to cut along underside of tail; clip off fins along edges.

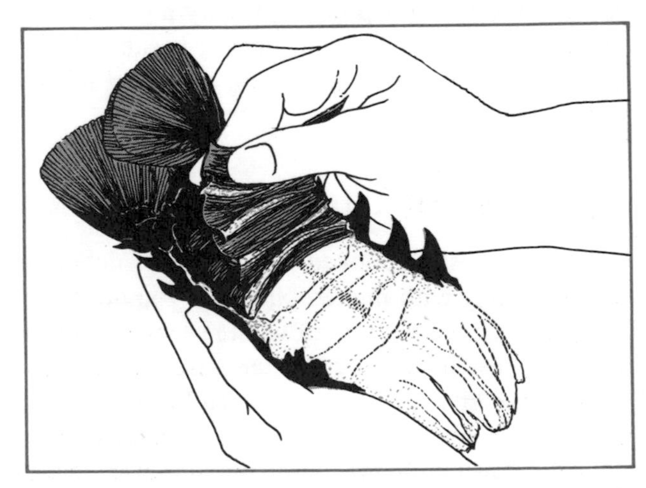

Peel back soft undershell, discard. Bend shell back, cracking joints to prevent curling while broiling.

Turkish Lobster Salad

The Turkish word for lobster is *istakoz;* the Turks also make this salad with shrimp, which they call *karidez*. Serve it as part of a buffet.

2 pounds lobster tails (or large shrimp, or some of each)
1 quart boiling water
2 bay leaves
1 teaspoon salt
½ cup olive oil
½ teaspoon dry mustard
3 tablespoons lemon juice
Fresh dill or parsley, chopped

Drop thawed lobster tails or shrimp into boiling water with bay leaves and salt; simmer about 5 minutes, or until flesh loses its translucent look. Drain and cool. Shell and cut lobster meat into bite-sized pieces; shell shrimp and split lengthwise, removing the sand veins. Marinate 1 to 2 hours in olive oil mixed with dry mustard and lemon juice. Arrange pieces on a serving platter and pour some of the marinade over top. Garnish lobster or shrimp with dill or parsley.

Lobster Salad

Here's a perfect salad for a luncheon. It is most attractively served in the cleaned and dried lobster shells.

Dice meat from 2 cooked frozen lobsters (1 to 1½ lbs. each); or about 1 pound of frozen lobster tails, boiled as directed on page 66; or use about 2 cups langostinas. Blend ¼ cup mayonnaise, ¼ cup sour cream, 2 tablespoons tarragon vinegar, 1 minced hard-cooked egg, 2 small chopped green onions, 1 tablespoon minced fresh parsley, ¼ teaspoon salt, and ¼ teaspoon pepper. Add lobster and blend; spoon into cleaned and dried lobster shells. Sprinkle paprika over top. Garnish with lemon slices and parsley sprigs. Recipe makes 4 servings.

Lobster or Crab Bisque

Creamy lobster bisque is best made just before serving; you can use cooked or canned lobster or crab meat.

2 tablespoons butter
1 medium-sized onion, finely chopped
1 celery stalk, finely chopped
About 2 tablespoons chopped parsley
½ bay leaf
4 cups milk
4 tablespoons flour
½ teaspoon salt
½ teaspoon seasoned salt
1 can (about 5 oz.) lobster meat, or 1 can (about 7 oz.) crab meat, or about 1 cup cooked lobster or crab meat

Melt 1 tablespoon of the butter in a frying pan and add onion, celery, parsley, and bay leaf. Cook, stirring occasionally, until vegetables are soft, but not browned (about 10 minutes). Blend in milk and bring to simmer over medium high heat. Pour through a fine wire strainer and discard the vegetables. (You can do this ahead; keep cold until ready to use.)

Melt the remaining 1 tablespoon butter in the frying pan and blend in flour, salt, and seasoned salt; gradually add the flavored milk, blending well. Add lobster meat or crab meat and cook, stirring, until soup boils and is thickened slightly. Ladle into bowls. Makes 4 servings.

Lobster Parmesan

Colorful lobster Parmesan resembles lobster Thermidor, but the preparation is much simpler. Serve in lobster shells or shallow bowls.

2 cooked frozen lobsters (1 to 1½ pounds each*), or about 1 pound lobster tails (boiled as directed on page 66), or about 2 cups langostinas*
1 can (10½ oz.) white sauce
3 tablespoons grated Parmesan cheese
1½ tablespoons white wine
Parmesan cheese (optional)
Fresh minced parsley (optional)
Parsley sprigs
Lemon wedges

Dice lobster meat. In a small saucepan, mix white sauce, the 3 tablespoons grated Parmesan cheese, and the white wine. Place over low heat and stir in lobster meat; remove from heat when lobster is heated through. Spoon warm mixture into clean, dry lobster shells. If you wish, top each with more Parmesan and a sprinkle of parsley and place under the broiler for 2 minutes. Garnish with parsley and lemon wedges. Makes 4 servings.

Lobster Tails Thermidor

Frozen lobster tails are used in this lobster Thermidor recipe. You combine the cooked lobster meat in the wine-flavored sauce and return it to the shells for browning and serving. The shells are shiny and bright because they are first heated in melted butter.

3 quarts water
1 medium-sized onion, quartered
2 whole cloves
½ cup sliced celery
1 bay leaf
6 frozen rock lobster tails (8 to 10 oz. each*), thawed*
¾ cup butter
⅓ cup dry sherry
⅓ cup dry white wine
⅓ cup flour
1½ cups milk
½ teaspoon salt
¼ teaspoon pepper
⅛ teaspoon nutmeg
Grated Parmesan cheese
3 fresh mushrooms, sliced, or 1 can (2 oz.) sliced mushrooms, drained
1 tablespoon salad oil or melted butter

Using a large pan, pour in water, add onion stuck with the cloves, celery, and bay leaf, and bring to a boil. Add lobster tails and bring to a boil again; skim off foam, simmer 6 to 8 minutes, or until tender, and remove from heat. Drain and cool. With scissors cut along the underside of the shell and pull it off (directions on page 66). Remove lobster meat from the shell and cut into bite-sized chunks. Wipe shells with paper towels to remove any moisture.

Melt ½ cup of the butter in a large frying pan and dip shells in the butter; heat for a minute, turning to coat both sides. (The lobster flavor permeates the butter and the shells acquire a nice sheen.) Remove shells, fan out tail fins, and arrange in a shallow baking pan. Add lobster meat to the remaining butter and sauté lightly, stirring. Pour in wine and cook down slightly. Set aside.

Lobster tails are filled with diced lobster in a delicate wine sauce and garnished with mushrooms to make lobster Thermidor, a festive entrée. Sourdough French bread is a good accompaniment.

In another pan, melt the remaining ¼ cup butter and blend in flour, stirring to make a roux. Blend in milk, salt, pepper, and nutmeg; stirring, cook until thickened. Pour the sauce over the lobster and wine and mix lightly. Spoon into shells. Sprinkle with grated cheese. Dip sliced mushrooms in oil or butter and arrange 2 or 3 slices on top of each. Bake in a moderate oven (350°) for 10 minutes or until hot. Makes 6 servings.

Lobster Newberg

Lobster Newberg is a simple way of serving cooked lobster meat in a sherry-flavored cream sauce. Slice the meat from about 1 pound lobster tails, boiled as directed on page 66, or from 2 average cooked frozen lobsters (1 to 1½ lbs. *each*), or use 2 cups langostinas. Place lobster slices (or the whole langostinas) in a saucepan containing 3 tablespoons melted butter seasoned with ¼ teaspoon salt, ¼ teaspoon pepper, ⅛ teaspoon paprika, and a dash of cayenne pepper. Cook just until heated through.

In another saucepan, heat to scalding point 1 cup half-and-half (half cream, half milk); stir in ⅓ cup dry sherry. Beat 2 egg yolks slightly; then beat in the hot cream mixture. Return to heat and cook, stirring constantly, just until slightly thickened (do not boil). Season with about ¼ teaspoon salt. Pour the sauce over lobster; heat through and serve the mixture over toast or in patty shells. Makes 4 servings.

Lobster à l'Américaine

The sauce that gives lobster à l'Américaine its delicate flavor makes use of vegetables, herbs, and both a liqueur and a wine. Use Northern lobsters, live if possible, for this recipe.

3 lobsters (1 to 2 lbs. each*)*
1 or 2 sprigs parsley
1 bay leaf
1 sprig fresh thyme or 1 teaspoon dried thyme
½ cup chopped onion
½ cup chopped celery
½ cup chopped carrot
1 tablespoon butter
1 tablespoon olive oil or salad oil
2 tablespoons Cognac
1 cup dry white wine
1 cup consommé
2 cups peeled, seeded, and diced tomatoes
2 tablespoons minced parsley

If possible, get live Northern lobsters for this dish. Split and clean as directed on page 65, reserving the tomally or liver (yellow part), and the coral or roe (pale or deep pink part), if any. Remove legs and break in half. (If you wish, you can discard the legs or save them for bisque.) Cut tail meat, shell and all, into 1-inch sections; crack claws of Northern lobsters. Make an herb bouquet by tying together in a piece of cheesecloth the 1 or 2 sprigs parsley, the bay leaf, and thyme. Use a long string so the bouquet can easily be removed from the pan. Cook the onion, celery, carrot, and herb bouquet in the butter and oil until wilted. Add lobster pieces, including legs, if used, and claws; cook until shells turn red. (If precooked lobster is used, cook just until heated through.) Add Cognac and flame. Remove lobster and keep warm. Add wine, consommé, and tomatoes to pan; simmer for 15 minutes. Discard bouquet; add lobster, tomally, and coral; heat well. Serve in a hot dish, sprinkling the top with the parsley. Makes 6 servings.

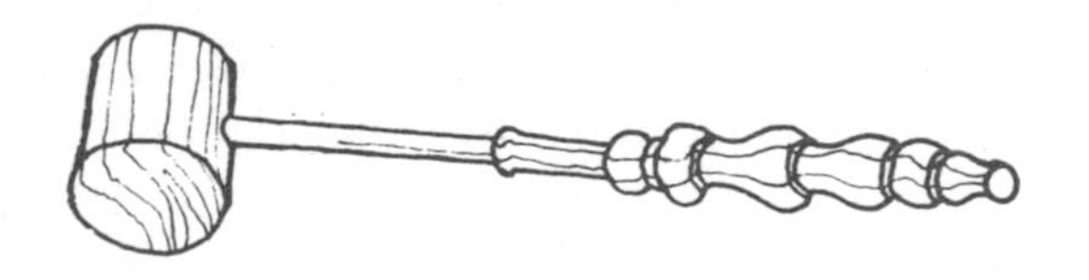

Beef Lobster Kebabs

Meat for six cooks on two skewers when you use a giant shish kebab combination of beef sirloin or top round steak cubes, and lobster tails.

If you use round steak you may want to prepare it with instant meat tenderizer, following the directions given on the container. Serve these kebabs with a special Béarnaise sauce.

3 frozen lobster tails (about 8 oz. each*), thawed and split lengthwise*
1½ to 2 pounds top sirloin or top round steak cut into 2-inch cubes
⅓ cup dry white wine
⅓ cup salad oil
1 tablespoon lemon juice
Lemon wedges
Tomato Béarnaise sauce (recipe follows)

Thread skewers, alternating lobster with beef cubes by wrapping the lobster tail around a piece of beef and threading the skewer through the thick end of lobster tail, the beef cube, then the end of the lobster tail. You can put three of these combinations onto each of two long skewers. Grill over hot coals for 8 to 12 minutes, or until lobster meat loses its translucent look and beef is done to your liking. Baste while cooking with a mixture of the wine, salad oil, and lemon juice. Serve hot with lemon wedges and tomato Béarnaise sauce (recipe below). Makes 6 servings.

TOMATO BEARNAISE SAUCE:

3 egg yolks
1½ tablespoons tarragon vinegar
¾ cup butter, melted
½ teaspoon salt
½ teaspoon tarragon
3 tablespoons finely chopped parsley
2 tablespoons tomato purée

Combine in blender the egg yolks and vinegar. Turn blender on high speed and immediately pour in the hot butter in a slow steady stream. Add salt, tarragon, and parsley; whirl until blended, about 30 seconds. Mix in tomato purée. Makes about 2 cups sauce.

CRAB

Dungeness and Alaska King

Two principal kinds of crabs are available in our markets—Dungeness (market) crab and Alaska king crab.

Fresh Dungeness crabs can be obtained nearly the year around in the Northwest. In California, the season is from mid-November to late July, but the supply normally declines toward the end of the season; during the rest of the year only frozen or canned Dungeness crab is available.

For the finest and freshest flavor, Dungeness crabs should be kept alive until just before they are cooked and eaten. The flavor advantages are quite pronounced when the crab is used in a dish that requires further cooking, for it is almost impossible to avoid overcooking when you reheat crab already cooked at the market. When in season, many West Coast markets have live crabs, or can order them for you if you call several days in advance to make arrangements.

In addition to the live crabs, markets also sell whole Dungeness crab cooked in the shells, fresh cooked crab meat, frozen cooked meat, and canned crab meat. A whole crab weighs 1¾ to 3½ pounds; a medium-sized one is about 2 or 2½ pounds. If you buy whole crab and plan to use the meat for salads or other dishes, you will have to buy about 4 pounds whole crab to get 1 pound of crab meat. A cup of crab meat, loosely packed into the cup, weighs about 6 ounces.

King crab from Alaska is available cooked and frozen in our markets. These large crabs weigh from 6 to 20 pounds, and the biggest ones measure 6 feet from the tip of one leg to the tip of the opposite leg. Frozen king crab legs, cooked in the shells, can be purchased in most markets, along with the frozen crab meat and canned meat. Specialty fish markets sometimes sell the whole crabs, cooked and frozen.

Because the meat of king crab is always cooked when you buy it, care must be taken when you reheat it not to cook the meat further; cook only until heated through. Plan on about ¾ pound king crab legs in shells for each serving.

HOW TO CLEAN AND CRACK LIVE DUNGENESS CRAB

For the finest flavor in all hot crab dishes, the live crab should be cracked and cleaned before it is cooked; in this way, the crab is only cooked once.

You'll need a heavy knife or cleaver, and a mallet or hammer. Rubber gloves are not essential, but will protect your hands from cuts and scratches (the pieces of broken shell can be sharp). Work on a board near the sink.

1) Grasp the live crab from the rear, getting a good hold on the last 1 or 2 legs of either side; place crab with back on cutting board.

2) Position a heavy, sharp knife in the direct center of the crab, between the legs. Hit the back of the knife with a hard, quick blow to kill the crab instantly.

3) Get a firm hold on a front claw and twist off where it joins the body; repeat with the other claw and legs. Scrub claws and rinse well; set aside.

4) Pull off the top shell (pry with knife if necessary). Remove the gills and spongy parts under the shell, saving creamy crab butter; wash body and leg pieces well.

5) Hold each leg and claw piece on its edge and crack the shell with a mallet to open each section. The meat can then be lifted out easily.

6) Tap the back of the knife with the mallet to cut the body cavity, first in half, then each half into several chunks. Rinse away any loose shell pieces.

HOW TO COOK LIVE DUNGENESS CRAB

When you want cooked crab meat to use in salads or other chilled dishes, you can buy whole, cooked crabs or crab meat; but for best flavor, buy live crabs and cook them this way:

In a large kettle, heat about 8 quarts water (enough for 2 or 3 crabs) to boiling with 2 tablespoons salt. Grasp the live crabs as shown in step 1, on page 73, and drop into the boiling water. Cover the pan and simmer for 15 to 25 minutes (depending on size) after the water returns to boiling. Lift out with tongs and cool until you can handle. Crack and clean each crab as directed for the live crab, steps 3 through 6 on page 73.

HOW TO SERVE CRACKED DUNGENESS CRAB

When cracked crab is the entrée for an informal supper, keep the rest of the menu simple—a green salad or vegetable soup to start and crusty French bread with the crab. You may want to serve a sauce or dip to accompany the crab.

If you buy the largest crabs available (2½ to 3½ pounds each), you can estimate that a crab will serve two people quite generously. If the crabs you buy are small, better allow one crab per person. Have the fresh cooked crabs cleaned and and cracked at the market where you buy them, or cook, clean, and crack the crabs yourself (follow directions above and on page 73).

Arrange the cracked crabs on a large serving tray; you might place them on a mound of cracked ice if the tray is deep enough to collect the water as the ice melts. Furnish your guests with plenty of napkins and have dishes near each place for the discarded shells; finger bowls or hot, damp towels will be appreciated, too. The following four sauces are especially good with cracked crab:

CRAB SAUCE WITH SOY:

Combine ⅛ pound (4 tablespoons) melted butter or margarine, 3 tablespoons lemon juice, 1 teaspoon finely minced chives or green onion tops, 1 teaspoon minced parsley, 1 teaspoon soy sauce, dash of liquid hot-pepper seasoning, and ¼ teaspoon finely minced fresh tarragon or a small pinch of dried tarragon crumbled between your fingers. Serve warm. Makes about ½ cup.

LEMON MAYONNAISE:

In the container of your blender, put 1 egg, 2 tablespoons lemon juice, 1 tablespoon white wine vinegar, 1 teaspoon sugar, 1 teaspoon dry mustard, ½ teaspoon salt, and ½ teaspoon grated lemon peel. Blend until smooth (just a few seconds). With blender turned on, gradually pour in 1 cup salad oil in a slow steady stream and blend until smooth. (If you have no blender, follow the same procedure using a wire whisk.) Turn into a serving bowl. Cover and then chill. Makes about 1¼ cups.

GREEN MAYONNAISE:

Mix together ¼ cup mayonnaise, ½ cup commercial sour cream, 2 teaspoons lemon juice, ⅛ teaspoon crumbled dried tarragon, ¼ teaspoon salt, and 1 clove garlic, mashed. Mix in ¼ cup finely chopped watercress, ¼ cup finely chopped spinach, and ¼ cup finely chopped parsley. Cover and chill. Makes about 1½ cups sauce.

RÉMOULADE SAUCE:

Mix 2 tablespoons finely chopped chives, 2 tablespoons finely chopped capers, 2 tablespoons finely chopped dill pickle, and 2 tablespoons finely chopped parsley into 1 cup mayonnaise. Makes about 1½ cups.

HOW TO CLEAN AND CRACK LIVE DUNGENESS CRAB

1. To crack live crab, grasp crab from rear; holding one or two legs firmly, place back-side-down on board.

2. Position heavy, sharp knife in direct center of crab between legs; hit knife hard to kill crab instantly.

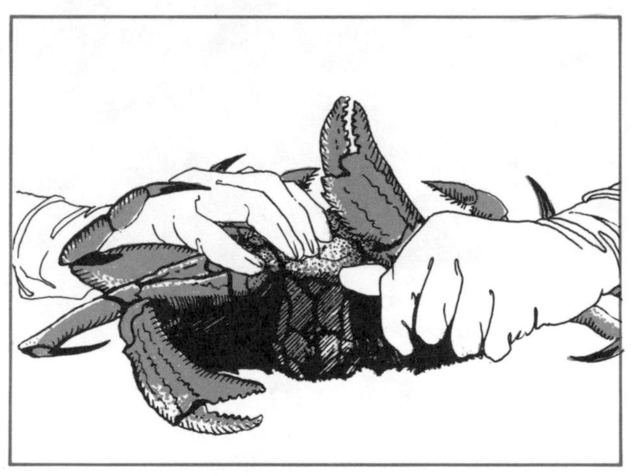

3. Get a firm hold on a front claw; twist off where it joins body; repeat with other claws and legs.

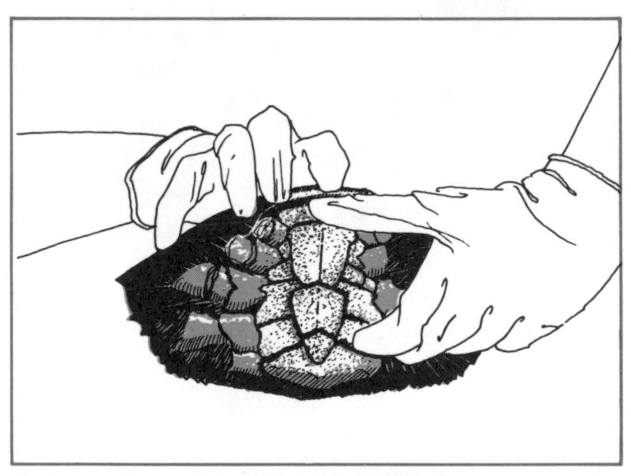

4. Pull off top shell (pry with knife, if necessary). Remove gills and spongy parts; save creamy crab butter.

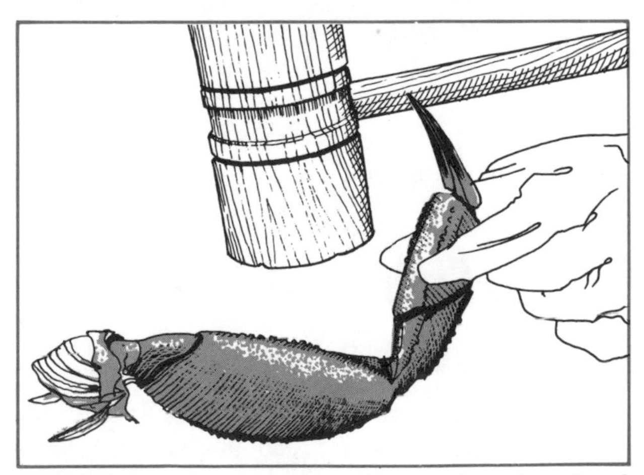

5. Hold each leg and claw piece on its edge. Crack shell with mallet or hammer to open up each section.

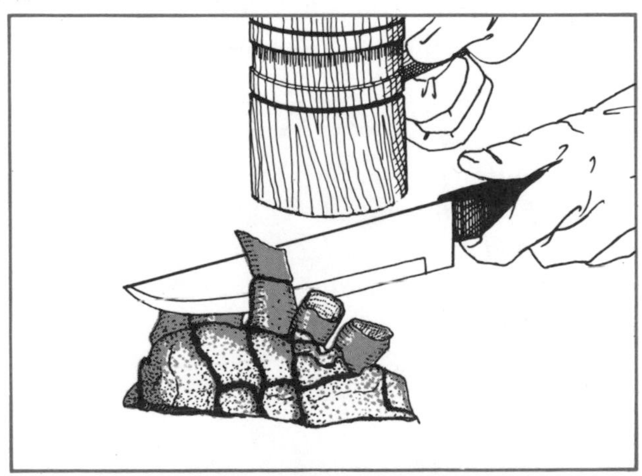

6. Tap back of knife with mallet to cut body cavity first in half, then each half into several chunks.

Serve marinated cracked crab to eat with the aid of a pick, fork, and fingers; afterward, have ready finger bowls or hot, moist towels. A green salad, French bread, and wine make good accompaniments.

Marinated Cracked Crab

Live Dungeness crab acquires robust flavor when prepared according to this recipe.

2 medium-sized live Dungeness crabs
½ cup salad oil
½ cup white wine vinegar
½ cup dry white wine
¾ teaspoon dry mustard
1 small clove garlic, minced or mashed
1 teaspoon salt
⅛ teaspoon white pepper or dash liquid hot-pepper seasoning
1 egg

Boil, clean, and crack live crabs as directed on pages 71-73. Combine in a bowl salad oil, vinegar, wine, mustard, garlic, salt, and pepper. Break in the egg, and mix with a fork until blended. Add the crab pieces in shells. Cover the dish and marinate in the refrigerator for 1 hour, mixing several times. To serve, lift the crab pieces out of the marinade and serve in large bowls or plates. Furnish small forks or picks, and offer finger bowls or damp towels. Makes 4 servings.

Cracked Crab in Spicy Tomato Sauce

Live Dungeness crabs are recommended for marinated cracked crab, but whole cooked crabs may also be served this way.

2 cups tomato catsup
1 cup water
3 whole cloves
1 teaspoon seasoned salt
½ teaspoon thyme
½ teaspoon sugar
½ teaspoon monosodium glutamate
1 tablespoon Worcestershire
1 teaspoon prepared horseradish
1 bay leaf
2 large Dungeness (market) crabs, about 2 pounds each

In a large pan (at least 5 quarts), combine the catsup with the water, cloves, seasoned salt, thyme, sugar, monosodium glutamate, Worcestershire, horseradish, and bay leaf. Heat slowly, stirring occasionally, until it simmers. Clean and disjoint the live or boiled crabs; crack the shells of each piece or ask the fish dealer to do this for you. Rinse well in cool water. Add the crab pieces to the simmering sauce; bring back to simmering; reduce heat and cook about 25 minutes, if the crab were uncooked to start. (If boiled crab is used, cook just until heated through.)

Serve crab with the sauce that clings to shells; extra sauce may be served in small bowls at each place. Makes 2 to 4 servings.

Shellfish Cioppino

No one knows who gave this delicious fish stew its name, but it was probably invented in San Francisco by an Italian.

Cioppino is a flexible dish, intended to make use of what the fisherman's catch provides. This recipe calls for shellfish in their shells and for live crab, which connoisseurs agree is necessary for the ultimate in cioppino flavor. (See pages 71-73 for directions on how to manage a live crab.) If you prefer, you can make the stew easier to eat by shelling the shrimp and clams and using cooked crab meat. Cook the shelled fish only about 15 minutes.

1 large onion, sliced
1 bunch green onions, including part of the tops, sliced
1 green pepper, seeded and diced
2 whole large cloves garlic
⅓ cup olive oil or salad oil
⅓ cup chopped parsley
1 can (1 lb.) tomato purée
1 can (8 oz.) tomato sauce
Tomato sauce can of white or red wine, or water
Tomato purée can of water
Half a bay leaf
3 teaspoons salt
¼ teaspoon pepper
⅛ teaspoon rosemary
⅛ teaspoon thyme
2 medium-sized Dungeness crabs
1 dozen fresh clams in shells
1 pound fresh prawns or large shrimp in shells

In a Dutch oven or a frying pan that has a cover, sauté the onion, green onion, green pepper, and garlic in olive oil about 5 minutes. Add the parsley, tomato purée, tomato sauce, wine, and water (or use all water), and all the seasonings. Cover and simmer about an hour. Remove the garlic. (You can do this much ahead if you wish.)

Clean and crack the live Dungeness crabs (see pages 71-73), or have this done at your fish market shortly before you plan to cook them; arrange crab pieces in the bottom of a large pan (at least 8-quart size). Scrub the clams well to remove any sand and put in on top of the crab. Cut the shrimp or prawns down backs with kitchen scissors, then wash out the sand veins; put on top of the clams. Pour on the hot prepared sauce; cover and simmer until the clam shells open, 20 to 30 minutes.

Serve in large soup bowls or soup plates, with some of each shellfish in each bowl. Makes about 6 servings. Sourdough French bread and a green salad are good accompaniments.

CRAB CIOPPINO:

Omit the clams and prawns or shrimp in the recipe above and use 4 Dungeness crabs.

Crab Pilaf

Greek in origin, the excellence of crab pilaf depends upon the use of uncooked crab; the cracked crab cooks with the rice.

2 medium-sized live Dungeness crabs
½ cup olive oil
1 medium-sized onion, sliced
2 cups water
1 can (1 lb.) tomatoes
1½ teaspoons salt
¼ teaspoon pepper
1 cup long grain rice, uncooked
3 tablespoons chopped fresh mint leaves or 1 tablespoon dry mint

Crack the live crabs as directed on page 71. Heat the olive oil in a Dutch oven or large frying pan with a tight-fitting lid. Sauté the onion until soft. Add the water, and press the tomatoes through a strainer into pan. Add salt and pepper, bring to a boil, and add the rice, crab pieces, and mint. Reduce heat; cover and simmer very slowly about 45 minutes, or until rice is tender.

Serve with picks for the diners to extricate the crab meat from shells; later offer finger bowls or damp towels to your guests. Makes 4 servings.

Crab and Cheese Puff

A layer of bubbling cheese tops delectable red and green-flecked crab puff entrée.

4 slices bread
1½ cups crab meat
½ cup finely sliced celery
3 tablespoons finely sliced chopped green onions (white part only)
2 tablespoons chopped pimiento
2 tablespoons chopped fresh parsley
¼ cup mayonnaise
1 tablespoon lemon juice
1 teaspoon prepared mustard
Salt to taste (about ½ teaspoon)
5 slices sharp process cheese
2 eggs
1 cup milk

Trim crusts from bread slices and arrange in bottom of buttered large baking dish (about 2-quart size). Combine crab meat, celery, onion, pimiento, parsley, mayonnaise, lemon juice, mustard, and salt. Spread evenly over bread slices. Arrange cheese on top. Beat together eggs and milk, and carefully pour over mixture in baking dish. Cover and bake in a moderately slow oven (325°) for 35 to 40 minutes. Remove cover and bake 10 minutes longer to brown top. Serve immediately. Makes about 6 servings.

Crab and Mushroom Supreme on Muffins

Fresh crab meat and sautéed mushrooms in a sherried sour cream sauce are spooned over toasted muffins for an elegant hot supper sandwich. You might accompany it with hot whole artichokes and a salad of mixed greens and mandarin oranges.

¾ pound fresh mushrooms
3 tablespoons butter
Juice of ½ lemon
¼ cup dry sherry
½ pint (1 cup) sour cream
¾ pound fresh crab meat or 2 cans (7½ oz. each) crab meat
3 tablespoons grated Parmesan cheese
4 English muffins
1 tablespoon minced parsley for garnish

Wash and slice mushrooms. Melt 1 tablespoon of the butter in a large frying pan; add mushrooms and squeeze over the lemon juice; sauté a few minutes. Add sherry and let cook down until liquid is reduced one half. Stir in sour cream, mixing until blended in. Add crab meat and grated cheese and heat until hot through. Split and butter muffins, using remaining 2 tablespoons butter; then toast muffins lightly. Arrange muffins on a serving platter or individual plates and spoon crab sauce over them. Sprinkle with parsley. (You can substitute ¾ pound cooked small shrimp or 3 cans — 5 oz. *each* — shrimp for the fresh crab meat in this recipe.) Makes 4 servings.

Crab Tetrazzini

Crab meat, clam juice, onions, and spices create a fresh taste in this version of Tetrazzini.

½ cup (¼ lb.) butter or margarine
1 cup thinly sliced green onions, including some of the tops
5 tablespoons flour
2½ cups chicken broth, canned or freshly made
½ cup clam juice
½ cup dry white wine
½ cup heavy cream
½ teaspoon basil
½ cup shredded Parmesan cheese
2 whole cloves garlic
½ pound mushrooms, sliced
Salted water
8 ounces noodles (spaghetti or vermicelli)
3 cups crab meat, fresh, frozen, or canned
Salt

Melt ¼ cup of the butter in a pan; add onions and cook, stirring, until soft. Mix in flour and gradually blend in chicken broth, clam juice, wine, cream, and basil. Cook, stirring, for about 3 minutes after sauce begins to simmer. Stir in ¼ cup of the cheese. Set the sauce aside.

Melt remaining butter in another pan; add garlic and mushrooms and cook quickly until lightly browned. Discard the garlic. Also bring to a boil a quantity of salted water; add the noodles and cook just until tender to bite, but not soft; drain.

Combine the sauce, mushrooms, noodles, and crab (save a few whole pieces for garnish if you like), and season with salt to taste. Pour into a large shallow casserole or individual casseroles. Top with reserved crab pieces and sprinkle with remaining cheese.

Bake in a moderately hot oven (375°) until bubbling; allow 15 minutes for the large casserole or 8 minutes for the small ones. Broil top until lightly browned. Makes 6 to 8 servings.

King Crab on the Half Shell

Broiled king crab legs on the half shell can be served with sour cream and French fries for a special but easy family dinner.

4 Alaska king crab legs (approximately 3 lbs.)
¼ cup (4 tablespoons) melted butter or margarine
Seasoned salt to taste
1 lemon
Parsley for garnish
Sour cream

Let crab legs thaw if frozen; then break them at the joints. (It is a good idea to wear gloves when you do this because the shell has many sharp points.) With scissors cut down both sides of each shell and lift off the upper half, leaving meat on lower half shell. Arrange the crab legs in their half shells on a baking pan and brush crab meat with melted butter. Sprinkle with seasoned salt to taste. Place about 6 inches below the broiler and broil for 5 minutes, or until hot through. Serve several pieces (about 1 whole leg) to each person. Garnish each serving with a wedge of lemon and parsley, if desired. Pass sour cream in a bowl. Makes 4 servings.

Crab Meat Patties

The pure flavor of crab comes through deliciously in little patties.

About 20 salted soda crackers
2 cups fresh or frozen crab meat, or 2 cans (7½ oz. each*) crab meat*
4 teaspoons Worcestershire
⅛ teaspoon liquid hot-pepper seasoning
3 tablespoons chopped parsley
1½ teaspoons prepared mustard
3 tablespoons mayonnaise
1 egg
3 tablespoons butter or margarine
Chopped parsley and lemon wedges

Finely crumble the soda crackers into a bowl; you should have 1 cup of crumbs. Thaw frozen crab or drain the canned crab; flake the crab meat into bowl with the crumbs. Add the Worcestershire, hot-pepper seasoning, parsley, mustard, and mayonnaise. Stir until blended. Add egg and stir until the egg is well blended in. Shape with your hands into about 8 patties. In a frying pan, heat 2 tablespoons of the butter. Put in the crab meat cakes and cook over medium heat (about 350° in an electric frying pan) until browned on both sides (about 3 minutes on each side). Add remaining 1 tablespoon butter when you turn cakes. Serve with additional chopped parsley on top and wedges of lemon. Makes 4 servings.

Elegant Crab Cocktail

½ cup catsup
¼ cup chile sauce
¼ cup tangerine or grapefruit juice
2 tablespoons lemon juice
⅓ cup finely sliced celery
1 tablespoon finely sliced green onions, with tops
1 teaspoon prepared horseradish
Two drops liquid hot-pepper seasoning
1 cup tangerine or grapefruit segments, chilled
1 cup avocado cubes or balls
2 to 3 cups crab meat
Lemon wedges

Combine catsup, chile sauce, tangerine and lemon juice, celery, onions, horseradish, and liquid hot-pepper seasoning. Chill several hours to blend flavors. To serve, add tangerines, avocado, and crab meat to catsup mixture. Spoon into seafood cocktail glasses or into lettuce cups, and serve with lemon wedges. Makes 8 to 10 servings.

Seafood Bisque

Condiments accompany this hearty seafood chowder, proportioned to serve a crowd.

1¼ cups butter or margarine
1 cup instant-type all-purpose flour
4 cans (7½ oz. each*) minced clams or 4 cups fresh minced clams*
½ gallon (8 cups) milk
1 pint (2 cups) half-and-half (half milk, half cream)
1 bunch green onions
2 pounds cooked crab meat
1 pound shelled cooked small shrimp
1 cup dry white wine
⅓ cup pale dry sherry
Parsley sprig for garnish
Assorted condiments: sieved hard-cooked egg yolks and egg whites (about 8 eggs), ¾ cup chopped chives, and ¾ cup chopped macadamia nuts

Melt ¾ cup of the butter in a 6-quart heavy-bottomed pan. Blend in flour and cook about 2 minutes. Drain liquid from clams and stir in the liquid, stirring until blended (reserve clams). Slowly stir in the milk and half-and-half, and cook until sauce is thickened.

Chop the onions finely, discarding half the green part. Using a large frying pan, sauté onions in the remaining ½ cup butter, cooking until limp. Add the crab, shrimp, and drained clams, and cook in the butter, stirring lightly, until seafood is hot through. Add seafood to the soup mixture and stir in the white wine and sherry. Heat just until hot through. Turn into a heated tureen or other large serving bowl or casserole. Garnish with a parsley sprig. Surround with small bowls of condiments. Makes 5 quarts or about 16 generous servings.

OYSTERS AND SCALLOPS

Shucked and Ready to Use

Oysters and scallops, removed from their shells and ready for use, are available in all our markets. Both types of shellfish are inexpensive and about as versatile as ground beef for preparing quick family entrées.

Most of our oysters are of the large Pacific variety; these originated in Japan, and the seed was brought to the Northwest in the 1920's. Since then, they have flourished on the Pacific Coast.

Pacific oysters are sold shucked, fresh or canned. The fresh ones are graded according to size: The choicest are extra small (over 144 oysters per gallon—sometimes called petit-points in markets), followed by small (97 to 144 per gallon), medium (65 to 96 per gallon), and large (not more than 64 per gallon).

Another variety of Japanese oyster, Kumamotos, are being raised experimentally in the Northwest, and some can be found in Northwest markets. These are of interest because they are smaller than Pacifics and are best eaten in summer. (Other oysters can also be eaten during summer, but are less firm and plump at that time.)

Our only native Western oysters are the baby Olympias, which once grew all along the Pacific Coast, but are now commercially grown only in the Puget Sound area. Shucked and packed in small bottles, they are expensive; however, their distinctive flavor makes them the connoisseur's choice for cocktails and canapés.

Small, choice Eastern oysters are imported from the East and Gulf Coasts for specialty fish markets in the West. They are available both shucked and unshucked; either way they are expensive, but considered well worth the price to anyone who savors raw oysters on the half shell.

Scallops in our markets are from the East Coast and Australia and are transported frozen. One large muscle from this shellfish, sometimes called the eye, is the only part that is used. The meat of scallops is very lean, tender, and slightly sweet in flavor. Popular ways of serving this shellfish call for scallop shells, prepared for use as individual serving dishes. These shells are available inexpensively in housewares stores and can be used for other foods as well.

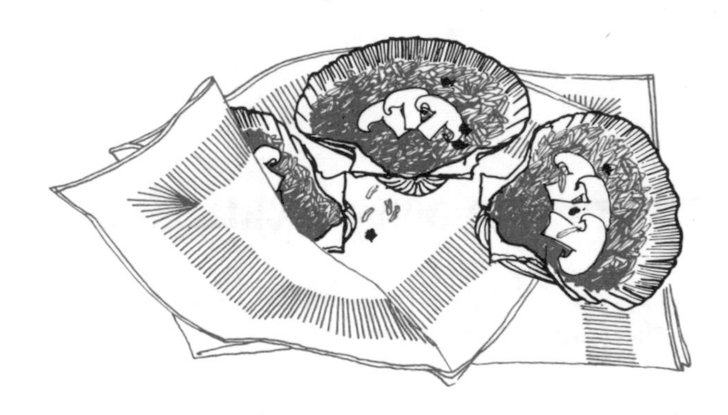

HOW TO POACH PACIFIC OYSTERS

This method of slightly precooking Pacific oysters, for use in cocktails and salads, makes them more acceptable in the opinion of many.

Cook the oysters in the simple poaching liquid given below for just a few minutes, until their edges curl; this plumps and firms them.

To make the poaching liquid, bring 2 cups water with 1 teaspoon salt and ½ teaspoon pepper to the simmering point in a small frying pan. Lower 1 to 2 cups oysters into the hot liquid and simmer (do not boil)over low heat for 4 to 6 minutes, or until oysters become plump and slightly firm; drain and chill. Try these poached Pacific oysters in any of the ways you usually serve raw Eastern oysters.

HOW TO POACH SCALLOPS

Some recipes call for poached scallops; here's how to poach them in a wine-flavored liquid.

Wash and drain 1¼ to 1½ pounds scallops. Put them in a pan with 1½ cups dry white wine (or use ¾ cup wine and ¾ cup water). Bring liquid to a boil, cover, reduce heat, and simmer for 8 to 10 minutes. Remove scallops and reserve the liquid for some of the sauces.

Oysters with Spicy Cocktail Sauce

Use poached Pacific oysters or raw Eastern oysters for these appetite whetters.

1 jar (10 or 12 oz.) Pacific or Eastern oysters
½ cup catsup
1 tablespoon lemon juice
1½ teaspoons prepared horseradish
1½ teaspoons Worcestershire
1½ teaspoons sugar
¼ teaspoon liquid hot-pepper seasoning

If Pacific oysters are used, poach if desired as directed on page 79; chill. Mix in a bowl the catsup, lemon juice, horseradish, Worcestershire, sugar, and liquid hot-pepper seasoning until blended; chill until serving time.

To serve, cut the poached Pacific oysters into bite-sized pieces (leave Eastern oysters whole). For each serving, place about 1 teaspoon of the sauce in the bottom of a cocktail glass. Place oysters over the sauce and spoon about 1 tablespoon of sauce over each serving. Garnish with lemon and parsley, if desired. Makes about 4 servings.

Oyster Salad

Capers and crisp celery complement the delicate oyster flavor in fresh tasting oyster salad. Serve it as a first course or luncheon salad.

1 jar (10 or 12 oz.) small Pacific oysters
1 teaspoon brown sugar
1 teaspoon prepared mustard
1 tablespoon lemon juice
1 teaspoon prepared horseradish
¼ teaspoon liquid hot-pepper seasoning
½ cup mayonnaise
1 cup crisp celery, diced
¼ cup capers, with juice

Poach oysters as directed on page 79. Drain; spread on a plate and chill thoroughly. Blend brown sugar, mustard, lemon juice, horseradish, and liquid hot-pepper seasoning into mayonnaise. Cut oysters into bite-sized pieces; add celery and capers; mix gently with seasoned mayonnaise. Makes 4 servings.

Scalloped Oysters

Scalloped oysters bake in a single layer between crisp, buttery soda cracker crumbs for a quick supper main dish.

Generously butter a shallow baking dish (10 to 12 inches in diameter, or square). Crush enough salted soda crackers to make 1½ cups fine crumbs; spread ¾ cup of the crumbs over the bottom of the baking dish. Melt ½ cup (¼ lb.) butter. Drain 2 jars (10 or 12 oz. *each*) fresh Pacific oysters; dip oysters into melted butter to coat well on all sides. Arrange oysters in a single layer over crumbs; drizzle with any melted butter remaining in pan. Sprinkle lightly with salt and pepper. Top with remaining ¾ cup cracker crumbs. Melt ¼ cup (⅛ lb.) more butter; drizzle evenly over crumbs. Place baking dish on an oven rack near the top of the oven; bake, uncovered, in a hot oven (400°) for about 15 minutes or until crumbs are well browned. Serve immediately. Makes 4 to 6 servings.

Hot Oysters on Toast

Crisp, hot oysters on a toasted bun make a tasty, unusual sandwich for supper. The sandwich takes on generous dimensions when you include toppings of tomato and dill pickle slices, chile sauce, and a squeeze of lime juice.

Drain 1 can (8 or 10 oz.) oysters. Dust with flour and allow to stand 15 minutes. Beat 1 egg with 2 tablespoons water. Dip oysters in egg, roll in cracker meal, and allow to stand 15 minutes more. Sauté in 4 tablespoons butter or margarine until a rich brown. Arrange oysters on 4 split, toasted, buttered buns. Top with dill pickle slices and sauce made by mixing ½ cup chile sauce with 4 teaspoons prepared horseradish. Serve with lime wedges, sliced tomato, and any remaining sauce. Makes 4 servings.

Nut-Crusted Fried Oysters

Crispy fried oysters have a subtle, nutty flavor when rolled in crumbs and nuts before frying.

¼ cup flour
¼ teaspoon black pepper
½ teaspoon allspice
2 jars (10 or 12 oz. each) large Pacific oysters (about 16), drained
2 eggs, slightly beaten
⅔ cup fine dry bread crumbs
⅓ cup finely chopped walnuts
4 tablespoons butter or margarine for frying

Combine flour with pepper and allspice. Roll drained oysters in flour mixture; let stand 15 minutes; then roll in beaten egg. Combine bread crumbs and walnuts. Roll oysters in bread crumb-nut mixture. Let stand another 15 minutes before cooking. Melt butter or margarine in a large heavy frying pan over medium heat and brown oysters about 4 minutes on each side. Serve oysters hot. Makes 4 to 6 servings.

Hangtown Pie

In this version of hangtown fry, oysters are coated with bread crumbs, fried to a crispy brown, and arranged on scrambled eggs in a pie shell.

8-inch pie shell, baked
1 jar (10 or 12 oz.) fresh oysters
Flour
1 egg, slightly beaten with 1 tablespoon water
Fine dry bread crumbs or cracker meal
2 tablespoons butter
2 tablespoons lard or shortening
4 eggs, slightly beaten
2 tablespoons light or heavy cream
Salt
Pepper
2 tablespoons minced chives
2 tablespoons butter

If pie shell is cold, place on a cooky sheet in a moderate oven (350°) while preparing other ingredients. Roll oysters in flour, dip them in egg and water mixture, drain briefly, and then roll in crumbs to coat all over. Fry in a mixture of the 2 tablespoons butter and lard or shortening until golden brown on both sides.

Meanwhile, blend slightly beaten eggs, cream, salt, pepper, and chives. Melt the remaining 2 tablespoons butter in a small frying pan, add egg mixture, and scramble until eggs are set. Spread scrambled eggs in bottom of warm pie shell. Arrange oysters on top. Cut in wedges and serve immediately. Garnish with lemon wedges and pickles, if you wish. Makes 5 servings.

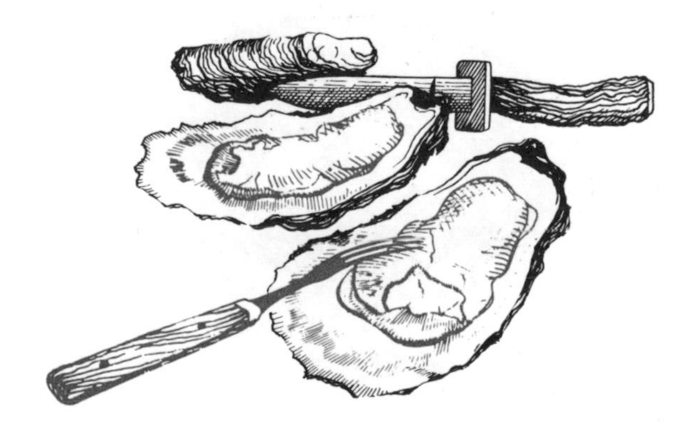

Creamed Lamb with Oysters

Lamb with oysters is surprisingly delicious; serve it for a simple family meal.

¼ cup butter or margarine
1 cup oysters, drained and chopped
½ pound fresh mushrooms, sliced
½ cup flour
½ teaspoon salt
⅛ teaspoon pepper
¾ teaspoon crushed marjoram
2 cups chicken broth
1 can (about 13 oz.) evaporated milk or 1½ cups light cream
2 to 3 cups cooked lamb, cut into bite-sized pieces
¼ cup chopped pimiento
Patty shells or crisp toast

Melt the butter in a large frying pan; add the drained and chopped oysters, and cook, stirring, for 5 minutes. Remove the oysters with a slotted spoon; set aside. Add mushrooms to the pan and cook about 3 minutes. Stir in the flour, salt, pepper, and marjoram; cook, stirring, until bubbly. Remove from heat and gradually stir in the chicken broth and evaporated milk or cream. Cook, stirring, until thickened. Add the lamb and pimiento; cook over low heat about 5 minutes. Return oysters to the pan and heat about 3 minutes. Serve in patty shells or on cut slices of crisp, hot toast. Sprinkle with chopped parsley, if you wish. Makes 6 to 8 servings.

Oyster Chowder

This hearty chowder is made with potato, onion, salt pork, and lots of oysters.

1 long thin slice salt pork, diced (about ½ cup)
1 large onion, diced
1 cup hot water
1 large potato, peeled and diced
1 teaspoon salt
1 or 2 jars (about 10 oz. each*) fresh Pacific oysters, quartered*
2 cups half-and-half (half milk, half cream)
Additional salt and pepper or cayenne to taste

In a large, heavy pan, fry the salt pork until lightly browned. Add the onion and sauté slowly until soft but not browned (about 5 minutes). Drain off fat, leaving salt pork and onion in the pan. Add water, potato and salt; cover pan and cook until potato is tender, about 7 minutes. Reduce heat to low; add oysters, and cook just until the edges curl, about 5 minutes. Meanwhile in the top of a double boiler (or another pan over low heat), heat the half-and-half to the scalding point; stir into the oyster mixture. Remove from heat; add salt, and pepper or cayenne to taste, and serve immediately. (If it is necessary to delay serving, keep soup over lowest heat on range or in top of a double boiler.) Makes about 4 to 6 servings.

Baked Oyster Custard

Oyster custard is as good for breakfast as for lunch or dinner. Serve it with toast or crackers.

1 jar (10 or 12 oz.) fresh *oysters*
1½ tablespoons butter or margarine
3 eggs, slightly beaten
1 cup light cream
¼ teaspoon salt
Dash black pepper
2 teaspoons sherry or lemon juice
⅛ teaspoon thyme
4 salted soda crackers, crumbled

Put the oysters in a pan and bring to a boil in their own liquid; add the butter or margarine and set aside. Beat the eggs and cream together lightly; add the salt, pepper, sherry or lemon juice, thyme, and crackers. Stir in the oysters and their liquid; pour into 6 individual buttered baking dishes.

Set the dishes in a pan of hot water (about an inch deep) and bake the custards in a moderately slow oven (325°) about 25 minutes, or until a knife blade inserted in the center of the custard comes out clean. Makes 6 servings.

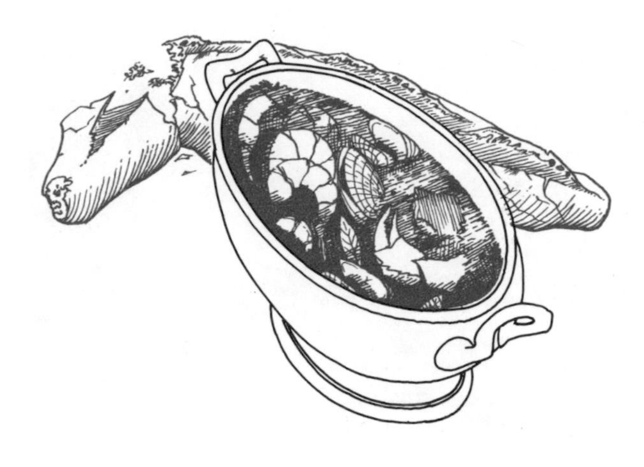

Oysters Meunière in French Rolls

Very small Pacific oysters (called petit-point) are ideal for savory individual oyster loaves, but you can use larger oysters instead.

4 French rolls
3 tablespoons soft butter
1 tablespoon lemon juice
1 tablespoon dry white wine
¼ teaspoon salt
¼ teaspoon crumbled dried tarragon
1 jar (10 or 12 oz.) oysters, drained
2 tablespoons heavy cream
Parsley or watercress for garnish

Slice a "lid" off the top of each roll, and pull out most of the soft bread inside. Spread 2 tablespoons of the soft butter inside each roll and on the lids. Toast in a very hot oven (450°) until lightly browned. In a frying pan place the remaining 1 tablespoon butter, lemon juice, wine, salt, and tarragon. Add oysters (cut into bite-sized pieces, if necessary) to the pan. Heat until bubbly and oysters are cooked through, about 5 minutes. Spoon oysters into French roll cases, and cook down pan juices until reduced to ¼ cup. Stir in the cream and heat, stirring. Spoon over oysters, and garnish with parsley or watercress; arrange roll lids to the side. Makes 4 servings.

Shrimp-Oyster Creole

Oysters and shrimp are combined here to make a colorful and tasty creole casserole.

2 slices bacon, cut up
1 clove garlic, minced or mashed
2 medium-sized onions, sliced
1 cup celery and leaves, chopped
1 cup slivered green peppers
1 bay leaf
1 teaspoon chile powder
¼ teaspoon pepper
1 can (1 lb.) tomatoes
1½ cups water
1 tablespoon vinegar
¾ cup rice
1 teaspoon sugar
½ cup cooked or canned peas
½ pound shrimp, cooked
1 jar (10 or 12 oz.) oysters

In a large frying pan, cook bacon, garlic, onions, celery, and green pepper together until tender. Add bay leaf, chile powder, pepper, tomatoes, water, vinegar, rice, and sugar. Bring to a boil. Remove bay leaf. Pour mixture into a 2-quart casserole; cover, and bake in a moderately hot oven (375°) for 45 minutes. Lightly mix in peas and shrimp. Arrange oysters on top. Return to oven and bake uncovered for 10 minutes longer, or until the edges of the oysters begin to curl. Makes 6 to 8 servings.

Coquilles St. Jacques features scallops and mushrooms in a mild cheese sauce. Served in a scallop shell, the complete dish is broiled just long enough to brown the decorative border of potatoes.

Coquilles St. Jacques in Butter

For a simple version of Coquilles St. Jacques, serve poached scallops in parsley butter as a first course.

1½ pounds scallops, poached as directed on page 80, cut into large slices
½ cup (¼ lb.) melted butter
2 tablespoons chopped parsley
Paprika

Arrange the sliced scallops in 4 scallop shells or individual casseroles. Spoon 2 tablespoons melted butter over top of each filled shell. Sprinkle 1½ teaspoons parsley over each; then sprinkle them with paprika and heat in a moderate oven (350°) for 5 minutes. Makes 4 servings.

Coquilles St. Jacques in Cheese Sauce

An attractive and hearty dish of Coquilles St. Jacques combines scallops and mushrooms. Serve it for a first course or luncheon dish.

1 can (3 or 4 oz.) chopped mushrooms
1¼ pounds scallops, poached as directed on page 80, cut into pieces
2 tablespoons butter
2 tablespoons flour
¼ teaspoon salt
1 cup of the poaching liquid
½ cup shredded Cheddar cheese
2 cups mashed potatoes
2 tablespoons melted butter
1 egg, lightly beaten

Combine the drained mushrooms and scallop pieces in a bowl. In a medium-sized pan, melt the butter and stir in the flour and salt to make a roux. Slowly pour in the 1 cup poaching liquid, stirring and cooking until smooth and thickened. Add cheese and continue to stir until the cheese is melted. Add the mushrooms and scallops to the sauce and spoon this mixture into 4 or 5 scallop shells or in individual casseroles. Mix potatoes with melted butter and egg; pipe mixture around edge of shells with a pastry bag. Place shells in a moderately hot oven (375°) for 8 minutes or until cheese sauce begins to bubble. Makes 4 or 5 servings.

Scallops La Jolla

Depending on the size of servings, make scallops La Jolla a first course or a main dish.

3 pounds scallops
1½ cups dry white wine (or ⅓ cup lemon juice with 1¼ cups water)
2 tablespoons lemon juice
¾ pound fresh mushrooms, sliced
1 green pepper, diced
¼ cup (⅛ lb.) butter or margarine
½ teaspoon salt
Dash pepper
4 tablespoons flour
1 cup diced Swiss cheese
½ cup grated Romano or Parmesan cheese
1 cup heavy cream, whipped
About 2 tablespoons butter for topping
Paprika

Wash and drain scallops. Bring wine and the 2 tablespoons lemon juice almost to boiling; add scallops, mushrooms, and green pepper; simmer slowly for 8 minutes. Drain, saving liquid. Melt the ¼ cup butter; blend in salt, pepper, and flour until bubbly; gradually stir in liquid in which scallops were cooked; cook until thickened. Add Swiss cheese and ¼ cup of the grated cheese; stir over low heat until blended. Remove from heat and fold in whipped cream; stir in scallop mixture. Divide among 6 or 10 buttered individual baking dishes. Sprinkle with rest of grated cheese, dot with butter; sprinkle with paprika. Broil until browned.

Scallop Seviche

Scallops are delicious when "cooked" by the action of citrus juice. This Mexican dish, served icy cold in nests of lettuce, is ideal as a first course on a warm summer night. Heaped into avocado halves or scooped-out tomatoes, it makes a pleasant addition to a buffet.

Cut into small dice or coarsely chop 1 pound raw scallops. Cover with fresh lemon or lime juice; cover dish, and let stand in the refrigerator for a couple of hours or until scallops lose their translucence. Drain well and mix with 2 ripe tomatoes that have been peeled and seeded, then cut in small dice; 4 to 6 green onions, chopped fine; and 1 firm but ripe avocado, cut in dice. Season to taste with salt. Makes 8 servings.

If you wish, add freshly minced cilantro (also called Chinese parsley or fresh coriander), to give it authentic Mexican flavor, but remember it's an assertive herb and may not appeal to everyone. Another optional seasoning is minced peeled green chiles (the canned ones do nicely), Mexican hot sauce, or liquid hot-pepper seasoning.

Deviled Scallops

You can prepare sautéed deviled scallops in a very short time.

¼ cup dry white wine
1 teaspoon Dijon-style mustard
¼ teaspoon thyme
⅛ teaspoon ground sage
⅛ teaspoon salt
2 tablespoons butter
2 tablespoons chopped shallots
1 small clove garlic, mashed
1 pound scallops, washed and dried
Parsley

Mix together white wine, mustard, thyme, ground sage, and salt; set aside. Melt butter in a frying pan; sauté chopped shallots, garlic, and the scallops over high heat for about 4 minutes. Pour wine mixture over scallops; boil rapidly for 1 minute to reduce liquid. Garnish with parsley. Makes 2 or 3 servings.

Tarragon Butter-Sautéed Scallops

Spoon this scallop and mushroom mixture into individual shells or ramekins for serving.

6 tablespoons butter or margarine
½ teaspoon tarragon
3 tablespoons chopped shallots or onions
2 cups sliced fresh mushrooms
1 pound scallops, washed and dried
1 tablespoon dry white wine
Chopped parsley
Lemon wedges

Melt butter or margarine in a large frying pan over medium-high heat and add tarragon. Sauté shallots or onions and mushrooms until just tender; push to the side of the pan and sauté scallops on both sides a total of about 4 minutes. Sprinkle wine over the fish and cook 1 minute longer. Mix the scallops with the mushrooms and spoon into individual shells or ramekins, if you wish. Garnish with chopped parsley and a wedge of lemon. Makes 3 servings.

Broiled Scallops, Chinese

Broiled scallops can be hot appetizers for a party, or an entrée for a family meal.

½ cup salad oil or olive oil
½ cup soy sauce
½ cup dry sherry (or 2 tablespoons lemon juice with 6 tablespoons water)
½ teaspoon powdered ginger
1 clove garlic, minced or mashed
1½ pounds scallops

In a bowl large enough to hold the scallops, mix together the salad oil, soy sauce, and sherry; stir in the ginger and garlic. Wash and drain the scallops and put into the soy mixture in the bowl, stirring until they are completely covered with the sauce. Marinate for 1 to 2 hours.

Just before serving, remove the scallops from the marinade and impale on bamboo skewers, leaving a little space between scallops. Set on a broiler rack about 2 inches from the heat in a preheated broiler. Broil for 4 to 5 minutes, turning several times and basting with the marinade. Serve immediately. For appetizers, push scallops off the skewers onto a heated serving plate and stick with toothpicks. Makes 4 to 6 main-dish servings, or 36 appetizers.

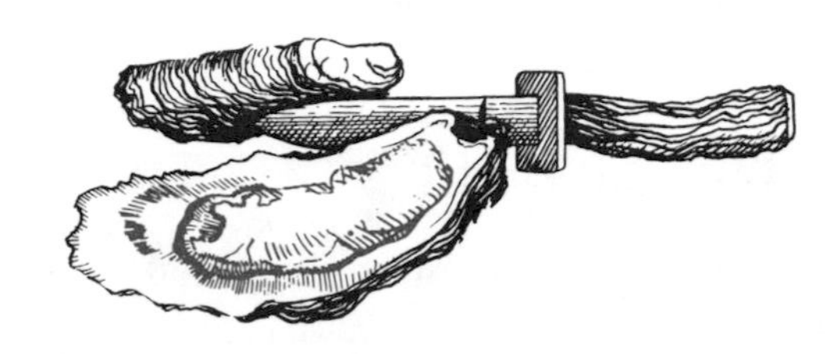

Cream of Scallop Soup

Serve cream of scallop soup as a first course with crisp crackers.

2 bottles (8 oz. each*) clam juice*
1 tablespoon butter or margarine
½ teaspoon Worcestershire
½ teaspoon dry mustard
⅛ teaspoon garlic salt
⅛ teaspoon celery salt
¾ pound scallops, cut up
2 egg yolks
1 cup heavy cream or half-and-half (half milk, half cream)
Chopped parsley or chives

Heat clam juice, butter or margarine, Worcestershire, dry mustard, garlic salt, and celery salt in a pan. When just boiling, add scallops, and simmer gently about 3 minutes. Beat egg yolks with cream or half-and-half; stir a little of the hot clam juice into the cream; then gradually stir the cream mixture into the remaining hot clam juice. Cook, stirring, about 1 minute, or just until liquid is slightly thickened. Garnish with chopped parsley or chives. Makes 4 servings.

CLAMS, MUSSELS, ABALONE

Gathering, Shucking, Cooking

Clam digging, gathering mussels, and diving for abalone are popular activities along the Pacific Coast. Half the enjoyment may be the excursion to the beach and the sport of finding these shellfish, but they are projects that sometimes pay off with the ingredients for a picnic at the beach or a feast at home.

CLAMS

There are numerous varieties of clams to be found on the sandy beaches, mud flats, and in the rocky areas of the Pacific. Each type of clam "terrain" requires different digging techniques. The best sources of information on clamming are the state fish and game departments of California, Oregon, and Washington. You will need to know the regulations regarding daily bag limits, seasons, and approved methods of digging. Most clams are more easily accessible at low (or minus) tides, so it is important to know how to use a tide table. Avoid areas where waters may be contaminated by sewage disposal.

In the summer months when the water is warm, there is an increase of small organisms in the water that may suffocate clams and poison persons who eat them. From May to November in California, certain beaches are quarantined, so look for postings. Although some clams are not subject to this poison, it is still a wise practice to remove the stomach contents if you use them during these months.

HOW TO CLEAN CLAMS

Before cooking the clams you dig, you will need to clean them. Most clams will release the sand and mud in their stomachs if you let them stand for 15 to 20 minutes in clean salt water (or ⅓ cup salt to 1 gallon tap water); change the water two or three times. Any dead clams should be discarded. When working with hard clams, gaping shells that do not close when touched mean that the clams are dead. With soft clams, there will be some constriction of the siphon, or neck, if the clam is alive when touched.

To remove a clam from its shell, you can use one of two methods: steaming or cutting. To steam clams, pour a little boiling water over the live clams and let stand a few minutes until the shells open; remove clams and plunge in cold water.

To open clams by cutting, insert a strong, thin-bladed knife between the shells near the thick end; run the knife blade around the shells until the muscles holding them together are cut. (Keep a bowl underneath the clams to catch the nectar.) Soft clams are easier to open because they do not have tight-fitting shells.

Once removed from the shells, the clam meat may be ground or minced. Tender whole clams or more tender parts of some large clams may be fried or used whole in a variety of recipes. Two large and choice clam varieties require some special handling — Pismos and razors:

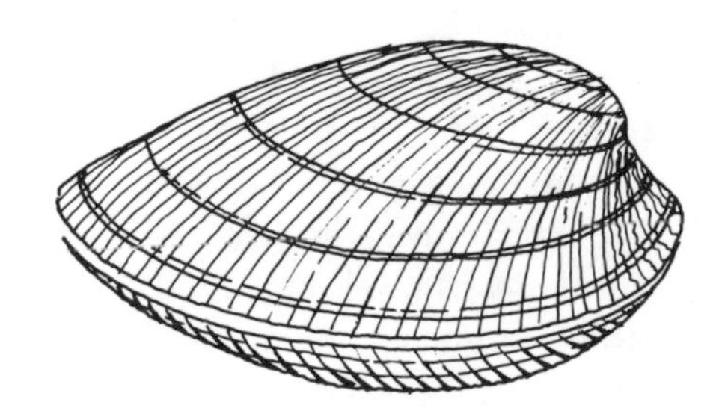

PISMO CLAMS

Cut this large clam from the shell as described on page 87. Rinse in cold running water to remove any sand; cut adductor muscles and lift clams from shells. The hinge or adductor muscles are tender and may be eaten raw in seafood cocktails. Cut out stomach; pound remaining firm parts of clam, which may then be fried.

RAZOR CLAMS

Remove meat from shells either by steaming or cutting (see page 87). Snip off the tip of the neck with scissors or sharp knife. Cut open the clam from the base of the foot to the tip of the neck. Remove the gills and digestive track (the dark parts of the clam). You may then fry the whole clam, put the meat through a food chopper, or mince it.

Clams are available commercially in several different forms. Small hard clams in their shells may be sold by the dozen or by the pound. The terms "littlenecks" and "cherrystones" are used in markets to refer to small hard clams which are frequently served raw on the half shell. Clams in the shells should be alive when purchased.

Fresh shucked clams (clam meat which has been removed from the shells) are available in some areas. Northwest markets sometimes have shucked razor clams. Canned whole clams, minced clams, clam juice, and clam nectar are available in all markets.

MUSSELS

These shellfish are abundantly available on the Pacific Coast. Easier to gather than clams, they are just as delicious. Some people are reluctant to eat mussels for two main reasons: First, taken at the wrong time of year, mussels can be lethally poisonous, so many shun them all year, not realizing that they are only temporarily dangerous; second, the meat is a bright red-orange color, which causes some people to react against it.

Mussels may be dangerous from May 1 through October. During these months, beaches are posted with quarantine signs. Do not eat (or drink the juice from) mussels from the Pacific Coast during this time, or at any time that such quarantine signs are posted.

At low tide, hunt for mussels where there are outcroppings of rock along the coast exposed to open, pounding surf. They are easy to see; mussels are crescent-shaped, thin, have a blue-black shell, and attach themselves to rocks with tough, brown, hair-like byssus or "whiskers." Pry them off the rocks with a crowbar or screwdriver. Don't take any home that have gaped open, for these are dead.

Clean mussels by scraping off the barnacles; then scrub them with a stiff brush under running water, and they are ready to be cooked (see pages 92 and 93).

HOW TO STEAM MUSSELS

Most recipes for mussels call for steaming them to open the shells. Place the mussels (cleaned as directed above) in a large covered pan with about half an inch of water; steam them until the shells open, about 5 minutes. The mussels can be served immediately with a pitcher of melted butter, or used in other recipes.

ABALONE

Abalone have a single, large shell. The edible portion is a foot-like muscle which clings to rocks. Skin divers pry them from the rocks along the California coast. Laws regulate the daily limit, seasons during which abalone may be taken, and the minimum size limits. To protect the resources, laws also prohibit shipping to other states abalone that have been taken in California waters. Frozen abalone steaks from Mexico and Japan, however, are sold in markets throughout the West. Generally these packaged frozen steaks have been pounded when processed, thus are ready for cooking after they have thawed.

Fresh abalone will live for several days if kept in a cool place and covered with a sack soaked in salt water. It is best to leave them in the shells until after you get home, provided the abalone is still alive (it will respond by slight movement when touched). Thereafter, the meat is perishable and should be eaten or refrigerated immediately.

To shuck and prepare live abalone, force a heavy wooden wedge or tire iron tip between the meat and the shell; move the wedge around until the muscle falls from the shell. Cut off the stomach on the side that was attached to the shell, being careful not to break the sac. Wash meat in cold water. Trim off tough dark portions around the edges of the meat with a sharp knife; these dark trimmings may be minced to use for chowder or fritters (see page 94). Hold meat down firmly on a board and, with a thin, sharp knife, cut across the grain into slices about ⅜ inch thick. Pound each slice with a wooden mallet until limp and velvety. Use light, rhythmical motion and pound evenly. If you prefer not to pound abalone, it may be put through a food chopper and minced.

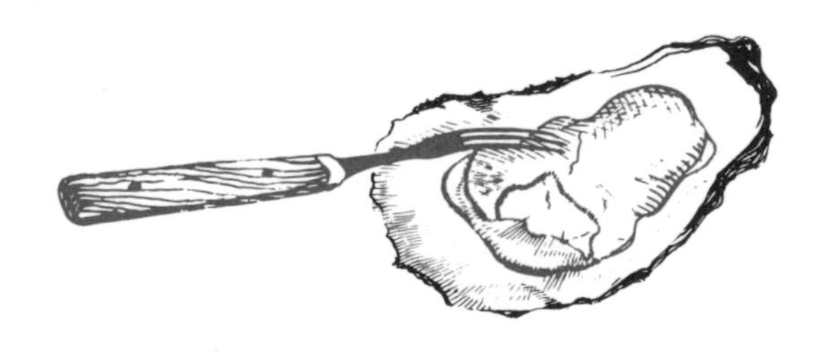

Sautéed Clams

Clean frying clams and prepare for cooking as directed on page 87; drain on paper towels. Dust each clam lightly with flour, shaking off excess. Heat enough salad oil (or half salad oil, half butter) in a frying pan to coat the bottom with about ¼ inch of fat. Sauté the clam pieces over high heat without crowding until lightly browned; it takes about 45 seconds for each side. Add more butter or salad oil to pan as needed. Remove clams to paper towels to drain; keep in a warm place until all are cooked. Salt if necessary.

Raw Clam Cocktail

Use small, tender whole clams or the adductor muscles of Pismo clams for this recipe.

Place clams (in large pieces or chopped) in a deep bowl and barely cover with an equal mixture of dry white wine and lime juice. Cover and chill for several hours. Season to taste with salt. Serve in small bowls or arrange in lettuce cups; garnish with tomato wedges.

Clam Fritters

Serve crispy clam fritters plain or with lemon.

¼ cup flour
½ teaspoon baking powder
1 egg
1½ cups ground clams
Salad oil (or half salad oil, half butter or margarine)
Lemon wedges (optional)
Salt (optional)

Thoroughly blend flour, baking powder, and egg with ground clams. In a wide frying pan, heat enough salad oil (or half salad oil, half butter or margarine) to coat the bottom with about ¼ inch of fat. Drop clam batter into hot fat by small spoonfuls, being careful not to crowd, and cook over high heat until fritters are browned on both sides (less than a minute to a side). Add more salad oil as required. Drain fritters on paper towels and keep warm until all are cooked. Salt to taste if needed. Makes about 20 fritters, each about 2 inches in diameter.

Pismo Clams in Shells

Large Pismo clam shells make handsome containers for this clam entrée, seasoned with mushrooms and wine-cream in sauce.

½ cup chopped green onions
½ pound sliced mushrooms
¼ cup (⅛ lb.) butter or margarine, melted
1 tablespoon flour
¼ cup heavy cream
¼ cup dry white wine or milk
½ cup clam liquid (reserved from Pismo clams, or canned juice)
2 tablespoons shredded or grated Parmesan cheese
2 cups ground Pismo clams (about 8 clams, 4½-inch size)
3 egg yolks, beaten
1 tablespoon lemon juice
Salt
½ cup fine dry bread crumbs
¼ cup grated or shredded Parmesan cheese
2 tablespoons melted butter or margarine
Mushroom caps, sautéed, for garnish (optional)

Cook onions and mushrooms in the ¼ cup melted butter or margarine over medium heat until onions are soft, and the liquid from mushrooms has evaporated. Mix in flour, and gradually add heavy cream, wine, and clam liquid. Cook, stirring, until bubbling. Add the 2 tablespoons Parmesan cheese and the clams.

Bring mixture to a boil, stirring. Blend some of the hot liquid with beaten egg yolks, and return yolks to pan. Cook over medium heat, stirring constantly, until thickened. Season with lemon juice and salt to taste, if needed. Mixture can be covered and chilled for several hours before using.

Spoon clam mixture into cleaned Pismo clam shells (this will be enough to fill 6 to 8 half shells). Mix bread crumbs with the ¼ cup Parmesan cheese and the 2 tablespoons melted butter or margarine. Sprinkle evenly over filled clam shells. Broil about 6 inches below heat for about 5 minutes, or until bubbling and heated. Garnish, if you like, with sautéed mushroom caps. Makes 6 to 8 first-course servings, or 3 to 4 main-dish servings.

Hearty Clam Chowder

Hearty clam chowder is likely to satisfy an appetite rather than create one. The mashed mixture of potatoes and other vegetables thickens the soup.

4 slices bacon, cut in small cubes
3 green onions and tops, chopped
5 medium-sized potatoes, peeled and cut in ½-inch cubes
2 tablespoons chopped green pepper
1 stalk celery, sliced
1 carrot, finely sliced
1 clove garlic, mashed or minced
2 cups water
1 teaspoon salt
½ teaspoon pepper
1 teaspoon Worcestershire
4 drops liquid hot-pepper seasoning
2 cups chopped or ground raw clams (with nectar)
1 pint (2 cups) half-and-half (half milk, half cream)

In a large heavy kettle, sauté bacon until crisp; add green onions and tops, potatoes, green pepper, celery, carrot, and garlic. Pour in water and season with salt, pepper, Worcestershire, liquid hot-pepper seasoning. Cover pan and simmer 15 minutes, or until potatoes are tender. Mash mix-

Steamed clams, presented in their shells with a lime wedge and a small bowl of melted butter for dipping, makes an unusual first course. The broth is spooned up after discarding the shells.

ture slightly with a potato masher. (If you prefer a thicker soup, mash potatoes well.)

In a separate pan, heat clams in their own nectar for 3 minutes, or until tender. Add clams to vegetable mixture; pour in half-and-half. Stir well; then heat just until piping hot, but do not boil. Makes 4 servings as a main course.

Steamed Clams in Wine Broth

Any variety of small tender clams that you dig or buy is suitable for this interesting first course. If you prefer this dish for a supper entrée, allow at least 20 to 25 clams per serving.

3 pounds clams in the shell
½ cup dry white wine
2 tablespoons butter
½ cup (¼ lb.) butter, melted
1 lime or lemon

Scrub clams thoroughly with a brush under cold running water. Using a large pan with a rack, pour in wine and add the 2 tablespoons butter. Arrange scrubbed clams on the rack. Cover and steam just until the shells open, about 6 to 10 minutes. Arrange clams in their shells in shallow soup bowls and pour over the broth. Pour melted butter into individual serving dishes or small tea cups and place one in the center of each soup bowl. Cut lime in wedges and garnish each butter dish. Makes 4 to 6 servings as a first course.

Sausage Clam Loaf

Chewy toasted English muffins make a good base for delicate sausage and clam loaf. Pass catsup for those who like it, and serve with a salad of mixed greens and hard-cooked eggs tossed with a tart oil and vinegar dressing.

1 pound bulk pork sausage
2 cans (7½ oz. each) minced clams
1½ cups cracker crumbs
1 medium-sized onion, finely chopped
3 eggs, slightly beaten
¼ teaspoon sage or poultry seasoning
1 teaspoon salt
¼ teaspoon pepper

Mix together sausage, clams (including liquid), crumbs, onion, eggs, sage, salt, and pepper. Spoon into a loaf pan (about 5 by 9 inches), and smooth surface. Bake in a moderate oven (350°) for 45 minutes. Drain excess fat from pan before serving or chilling. Serve sliced, either hot or cold. Makes 8 servings.

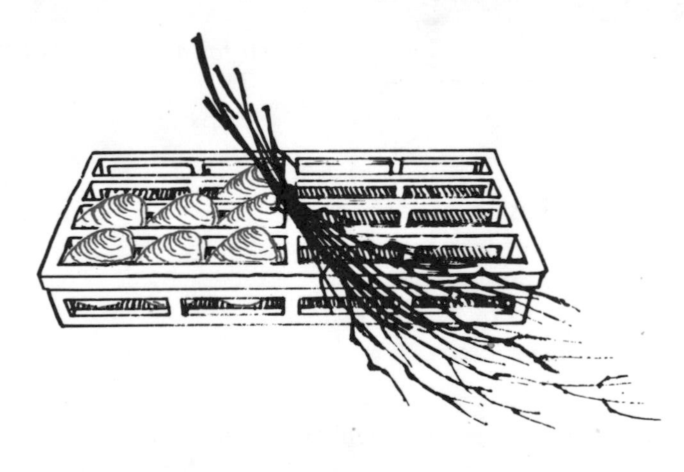

Shell Macaroni with Clams

Eggs, milk, and a small amount of macaroni give this dish a custard consistency. You can serve it as a main dish or as an accompaniment for broiled or roasted meats.

1 cup small shell macaroni
Boiling salted water
½ cup milk
1 can (11 oz.) condensed clam chowder
2 cans (7½ oz. each) minced clams
1 can (4 oz.) sliced mushrooms
6 eggs, slightly beaten
¼ cup chopped green onion
1 clove garlic, mashed
1½ cups shredded Swiss cheese

Cook macaroni in boiling salted water as package directs; drain. Mix cooked macaroni with the milk, clam chowder, clams, mushrooms (including liquid from clams and mushrooms), eggs, onion, and garlic; pour into a 9 by 13-inch greased pan. Sprinkle cheese over top. Bake, uncovered, in a moderate oven (350°) for about 40 minutes, or until set. Makes 6 servings.

Stuffed Mussels

Serve stuffed mussel shells for lunch or supper.

1 pint mussel meat (about 36 mussels)
1 cup chopped onion
½ cup (¼ lb.) butter
4 cups soft bread crumbs
¼ teaspoon freshly ground black pepper
½ teaspoon fines herbes (or mixture of thyme and marjoram)
¼ cup broth from cooking mussels
¼ cup pine nuts

Topping:

½ cup melted butter
1 cup fine cracker crumbs
¼ cup minced parsley

Steam large cleaned mussels until they open (directions on page 88). Remove meat and save broth. Measure 1 pint of the meat; chop (not too fine), and combine with the onion, which has been cooked in the butter. Add bread crumbs, pepper, fines herbes, and broth. Pack this stuffing into 18 of the largest mussel half shells; sprinkle each with pine nuts. Then sprinkle each with a topping made by combining melted butter, cracker crumbs, and parsley. Bake in a moderate oven (350°) until the top is nicely browned; serve at once. Makes 6 to 8 servings.

Moules Marinière

In the classic French dish, moules marinière, mussels are steamed with wine and seasonings.

1 gallon mussels in shells
Dry white wine or water
1 cup chopped onions
2 tablespoons chopped parsley
Pinch of crushed whole thyme
½ teaspoon pepper
Butter (optional)
Chopped parsley (optional)

Clean the mussels as directed on page 88. Put into a large covered kettle with about ¼ inch of the wine or water. Add the onions, 2 tablespoons parsley, thyme, and pepper. Cover the pan and steam for about 5 minutes, or until the shells open. Any mussel that fails to open should be discarded. Remove one half of the shell from each mussel; trim off the beard or byssus (this is most easily done with scissors) and arrange in soup dishes or on a serving plate. Strain and serve the broth with the mussels. You may melt ¼ pound of butter in the broth or accompany the broth with melted butter and chopped parsley. Makes 4 to 6 servings.

Abalone Steaks with Egg Sauce

Often called "fillets of the sea," abalone steaks are best when quickly pan-fried, not more than 1 minute on each side. The crumb-coated steaks may then be enhanced with quick soup sauce which complements the delicate abalone flavor.

1 can (10½ oz.) cream of chicken soup
½ cup milk
1 tablespoon finely chopped pimiento
1 tablespoon finely chopped parsley
1 tablespoon finely chopped ripe olives
1 hard-cooked egg, chopped
4 to 6 abalone steaks, fresh or frozen and thawed
2 eggs, slightly beaten
¾ cup seasoned cracker crumbs
3 to 4 tablespoons salad or olive oil
1 lemon

Pour undiluted soup into the top of a double boiler. Add milk and stir over direct heat until hot through and blended. Stir in pimiento, parsley, ripe olives, and chopped egg and place over hot water to keep warm. Pound abalone steaks if necessary (see directions on page 89). Dip in slightly beaten egg and then in cracker crumbs, coating lightly. Heat oil in a large frying pan and cook steaks quickly until browned, about 1 minute on each side. Spoon sauce over each steak and garnish with wedges of lemon. Makes 4 to 6 servings.

Abalone Stew

Hearty abalone stew is full of chewy abalone bits and tender potato cubes.

3 tablespoons butter or margarine
1 clove garlic, minced or mashed
1 medium-sized onion, finely chopped
1 can (8 oz.) tomato sauce
½ cup water
3 medium-sized potatoes, peeled and diced
½ teaspoon salt
¼ teaspoon pepper
½ pound abalone, pounded and sliced, cut in small chunks (see directions on page 89)

Melt butter in a large saucepan. Add garlic and onion and sauté until golden brown. Add tomato sauce, water, potatoes, salt, and pepper; simmer until potatoes are almost tender, adding ¼ cup more water if necessary. Stir in abalone and cook over low heat 5 to 10 minutes more, or until abalone is very tender. Makes 4 servings.

Abalone Parmigiana

A pizza-like topping makes a good looking way to serve crumb-coated abalone steaks. It is quite similar to the Italian way of preparing veal cutlets.

2 eggs
½ teaspoon salt
¼ teaspoon pepper
¾ cup fine dry bread crumbs
⅓ cup grated Parmesan cheese
6 slices abalone, fresh or frozen and thawed
⅓ cup olive oil
1 can (8 oz.) tomato sauce
2 tablespoons dry red wine
1 can (4½ oz.) sliced olives, drained
1 package (6 oz.) sliced Mozzarella cheese

Beat eggs with salt and pepper until light. Mix together the bread crumbs and grated cheese. Pound abalone if necessary (see directions on page 89). Dip abalone slices in the egg mixture, drain briefly, then dip in crumbs. Using a large frying pan, fry steaks in olive oil about 1 minute on each side. Arrange in a 9 by 13-inch greased baking pan. Mix together tomato sauce, wine, and olives and spoon over the abalone slices. Arrange ½ slice of cheese over each piece of abalone. Then place under the broiler until the cheese melts. Makes 6 servings.

Abalone Chowder

1 pound abalone trimmings, or pounded and sliced abalone, finely minced (see directions on page 89)
2 cups water
3 slices bacon, cut in small pieces
2 stalks celery, finely sliced
1 small onion, finely chopped
3 medium-sized potatoes, peeled and diced
2 carrots, sliced
2 cups water
1 teaspoon salt
¼ teaspoon pepper
Pinch of dried thyme (optional)
5 tablespoons butter or margarine
5 tablespoons flour
4 cups milk

Simmer abalone in 2 cups water for 1 hour, or until tender; drain. In a frying pan, cook bacon slowly; add celery and onion and sauté until clear. Cook potatoes and carrots in 2 cups water seasoned with the salt, pepper, and thyme until almost tender; drain. Melt the butter in a large pan; stir in flour and cook until bubbly. Gradually stir in the milk. Stir the cooked abalone, the bacon-celery-onion mixture, and the cooked vegetables into cream sauce. Heat; do not boil. Makes 6 servings.

INDEX

Abalone, 87-89, 93-94
  Chowder, 94
  Parmigiana, 94
  pounding, 89
  shucking, 89
  Steaks with Egg Sauce, 93
  Stew, 83
Albacore, 12-13, 34, 36
  barbecued, 38
    Oyster Topped, 39
    Sesame-Soy, 40
    Smoke-Barbecued, 39
  Curried Salad, 38
  how to prepare
    for poaching, 37
    loins, 37
    steaks, 37
  in Tomato Sauce, 39
  Poached with Cucumber Sauce, 38
  Stuffed Tomato Salads, 38
  with Lemon Butter, 39
  with Sour Cream Sauce, 38
Avocado-Masked Spring Salmon, 30

Bagels and Lox, 34
Baked
  Bass with Cheese Crumb Topping, 56
  Oyster Custard, 82
  Shad, 42
  Stuffed Salmon, 30
  Swordfish, Manzanillo, 45
Barbecued
  Albacore with Lemon Butter, 39
  Barracuda, 40
  Sablefish, 41
  Salmon Fillets, 30
  Salmon with Lemon Rice Stuffing, 31
  Swordfish with Basil-Garlic Baste, 44
Barbecuing, 5-6, 13
  see also names of individual fish and shellfish
Barracuda, 12-13, 35
  Barbecued, 40
  Casserole, 40
Basic poaching liquid, 7
Basil-Garlic Baste, 44
Bass, Giant Sea, 12-13, 21
  Poached with Rémoulade, 27
  see also Kelp Bass, Sand Bass, White Seabass
Beef Lobster Kebabs, 70
Bercy Sauce, 9
Bonito, Pacific,
  Braised, 54
  Fish Ragout, 55
  Stuffed with Tomatoes, 54
Braised Bonito, 54
Broiled
  Scallops, Chinese, 86
  Swordfish, Sinaloa, 44
Broiling, 5-6, 13
  fatter fish, 6
  lean fish, 6
  see also names of individual fish and shellfish
Brown Butter Almond Sauce, 10
Butter-Broiled Shad Roe, 42
Butterflied Shrimp Appetizer, 58
Butter-Sautéed
  Bass, 55
  Shad Roe, 42
Butter-Sautéing, 4-5, 13
  see also names of individual fish and shellfish
Buying guide for Pacific Coast fish, 12-13

Clams, 87-92
  cleaning, 87
    Pismo, 88
    razor, 88
  Fritters, 89
  Hearty Chowder, 90
  Pismo
    cleaning, 87
    in Shells, 90
  Raw Cocktail, 89
  Sausage Clam Loaf, 92
  Sautéed, 89
  Shell Macaroni with, 92
  Steamed in Wine Broth, 91
Cod, 12-13, 21
  Pacific cod, 21
    Fresh in Cream Sauce, 26
  salt-cod
    Basque Style, 26
    in Cream, 26
  Sea Stew, 27
  see also Lingcod (not a true cod)
Cold fish sauces, 10-11
Cooking methods for fish and shellfish, 4-8, 13
  barbecuing, 5-6, 13
  broiling, 5-6, 13
  butter-sautéing, 4-5, 13
  frying, 7-8, 13
  oven-frying, 7, 13
  poaching, 6-7, 13
  see also names of individual fish and shellfish
Coquilles St. Jacques
  in Butter, 84
  in Cheese Sauce, 84
Crab, 71-78
  Alaska King, 71
    on the Half Shell, 77
    preparation of, 77
  and Cheese Puff, 76
  and Mushroom Supreme on Muffins, 76
  Cioppino, 75
  Cracked in Spicy Tomato Sauce, 74
  Dungeness, 71
    cleaning, 71-73
    cooking, 72
    cracking, 71-73
    Cracked in Spicy Tomato Sauce, 74
    Marinated Cracked, 74
    Pilaf, 76
    serving, 72
    Shellfish Cioppino, 75
  Elegant Cocktail, 78
  Marinated Cracked, 74
  Meat Patties, 78
  Pilaf, 76
  Sauces
    Crab Sauce with Soy, 72
    Green Mayonnaise, 72
    Lemon Mayonnaise, 72
    Rémoulade Sauce, 72
  Seafood Bisque, 78
  Shellfish Cioppino, 75
  Tetrazzini, 77
Cracked Crab in Spicy Tomato Sauce, 74
Cream of Scallop Soup, 86
Creamed Lamb with Oysters, 82
Cucumber Sauces, 11, 30, 38
Curried Albacore Salad, 38
Curried Shrimp, 62
Curry Sauce, 9

Deviled Scallops, 85
Dill Butter, 58
Dilled Shrimp-and-Cheese Rolls, 60, 61

Egg Sauce, 9
Eggs Fried with Shrimp and Dill, 60
Elegant Crab Cocktail, 78
Estragon Sauce, 9

Fan-Tail Shrimp, 62
Fatter fish, 12-13, 35,45
  see also Albacore, Sablefish, Shad
Filbert-Crusted Sole, 15
Fillet of Sole
  Astoria, 15
  Bonne Femme, 17
Fillets, cutting and skinning, 53-54
Fish, 4-56
  buying guide, 12-13
  cleaning, 53
  cooking methods, 4-8
  cutting steaks, 53-54
  fatter fish, 12-13, 35-45
  filleting, 53-54
  freezing, 11
  lean, mild fish, 12-13, 20-27
  pan-sized whole fish, 12-13, 46-50
  Ragout, 55
  salmon, 12-13, 28-34
  sauces, 8-11
  scaling, 52-53
  skinning, 52-53
    fillets, 53-54
  sole, 12-13, 14-19
  sportfish, 12-13, 51-56
  stock (Fumet de Poisson), 9
    sauces, 8-9
  trimming, 52-53
  unique and fatter fish, 35-45
  Velouté Sauce, 9
Freezing fish or shellfish, 11
Fried Shrimp Balls, 59

Gravlax with Mustard Sauce, 33
Green Mayonnaise, 72
Grilled Sole, 14

Halibut, 12-13, 20
  Baked
    Fish Fillet, 25
    in a Crust, 22
    with Dill Stuffing, 23
  Barbecued, 22
  Basque-Style Steaks, 23
  California halibut, 12-13, 20
    Glazed Fillet of, 22
    Stuffed Baked, 24
  Curry, 22
  Pacific halibut, 12-13, 20
  Sea Stew, 27
  with Wine and lemon, 23
Hangtown Pie, 81
Hawaiian Shrimp Curry, 63
Hearty Clam Chowder, 90
Herb Mayonnaise Sauce, 10
Hollandaise sauces, 8-9
Horseradish Sauce, 29
Hot Oysters on Toast, 81
Hot Prawn and Grapefruit Cocktail, 59
Hot Shrimp with Dill Butter, 58

Iced Shrimp in Dill Marinade, 58

Kauai Fillet of Sole, 16
Kedgeree, 34
Kelp Bass, 51
  Butter-sautéed, 55
King Crab on the Half Shell, 77
  see also Crab

Lean, mild fish, 12-13, 20-27
  see also Bass, Cod, Halibut, Lingcod, Rockfish, White Seabass
Lemon Butter Sauce, 5
Lemon Mayonnaise, 72
Lemon Rice Stuffing, 31
Lingcod, 12-13, 21
  Baked Fish Fillet, 25
  Curried, 25
  Florentine, 25
  Grilled, 25
  Sea Stew, 27
  Stuffed Baked, 24
Lobster, 64-70
  à l'Américaine, 70
  Beef Lobster Kebabs, 70
  live
    boiling, 64
    broiling, 65
    cleaning, 65
    serving, 65
  Lobster or Crab Bisque, 67
  Newberg, 69
  Northeastern, 64
  Parmesan, 68
  precooked
    broiling, 66
    barbecuing, 66
  Salad, 67
    Turkish, 67
  Spiny Pacific, 64-65
  tails, 65-66
    boiling, 66
    broiling, 66
    Thermidor, 68, 69
  Thermidor, 68, 69

Mackerel, 12-13, 46
  Barbecued, 47
  Planked, and Mushroom Caps, 47
Marinated Cracked Crab, 74
Mayonnaise sauces, 10, 72
Mornay Sauce, 9
Moules Marinière, 93
Mushroom-Baked Sole, 16
Mussels, 86, 92-93
  Moules Marinière
  steaming, 88
  Stuffed, 92

Mustard Sauce, 33

Nut-Crusted Fried Oysters, 81

Oil and Lemon Sauce, 45
Oven-Fried Salmon, 33
Oysters, 79-83
Baby Olympias, 79
Baked Custard, 82
Chowder, 82
Creamed Lamb with, 82
Eastern, 79
Hangtown Pie, 81
Hot on Toast, 81
Kumamotos, 79
Meunière in French Rolls, 83
Nut-Crusted Fried, 81
Pacific, 79
poaching, 79
Salad, 80
Scalloped, 80
Shrimp-Oyster Creole, 83
-Stuffed Sole Florentine, 19
-Topped Albacore, 39
with Spicy Cocktail Sauce, 80

Paella Valenciana, 62
Pan-sized whole fish, 46-50
see also Mackerel, Smelt, Surfperch, Trout
Pescado en Concha, 16
Pismo Clams in Shells, 90
Poached
Albacore with Cucumber Sauce, 38
Salmon
with Cucumber Sauce, 29
with Horseradish Sauce, 29
with Shrimp Sauce, 29
Poaching, 6-7, 13
basic poaching liquid, 7
see also individual names of fish and shellfish
Portugaise Sauce, 10

Raw Clam Cocktail, 89
Rémoulade Sauce, 10, 72
Rockfish, 12-13, 20
Baked
Fish Fillet, 25
in Foil, 25
Two Rockfish, Stuffed and Baked, 24
Sea Stew, 26

Sablefish, 12-13, 35
Barbecued, 41
Poached in Tart Broth, 40
Smoked
Fish and Egg Bake, 41
Fish in Caper Cream Sauce, 41
Salmon, 12-13, 28-34
Avocado-Masked Spring Salmon, 30
Bagels and Lox, 34
Baked Stuffed, 30
Barbecued
Fillets, 30
with Lemon Rice Stuffing, 31
Gravlax with Mustard Sauce, 33
Kedgeree, 34
Oven-Fried, 33
Poached
with Cucumber Sauce, 29
with Horseradish Sauce, 29
with Shrimp Sauce, 29
smoked, 28
species, 28
Steaks
Baked in Lemon Cream, 32
with Grapefruit, 32
Swedish Salmon Bowl, 34
with Oysters, 32
Salt-Cod, 41
Basque Style, 26
in Cream, 26
Sand Bass, 51
Butter-Sautéed, 55
Sauces, 8-11
Barbecue, 55
Basil Garlic Baste, 44
Crab with Soy, 72
cucumber sauces, 11, 30, 38
Dill Butter, 58
fish stock sauces
Bercy, 9
Curry, 9
Egg, 9
Estragon, 9
Fish Velouté, 9
Mornay, 9
Green Mayonnaise, 72
Hollandaise sauces
with Cucumber, 8
with Shrimp, 8
Horseradish, 29
Lemon Butter, 5
Lemon Mayonnaise, 72
mayonnaise sauces
Brown Butter Almond, 10
Herb Mayonnaise, 10
Rémoulade, 10
Mustard, 33
Oil and Lemon, 45
Rémoulade, 10, 72
Shrimp, 18, 29
simple cold fish sauces
Cucumber, 11
Sauce Gribiche, 11
Tartare, 10
Teriyaki (Rockfish in Foil), 24
tomato sauces
Bearnaise, 70
Portugaise, 10
Sausage Clam Loaf, 92
Sautéed Clams, 89
Sautéing *see* Butter-Sautéing
Scalloped Oysters, 80
Scallops, 79-80, 84-86
Broiled, Chinese, 86
Coquilles St. Jacques
in Butter, 84
in Cheese Sauce, 84
Cream of Scallop Soup, 86
Deviled, 85
la Jolla, 85
poaching, 80
Tarragon Butter-Sautéed, 86
Seviche, 85
Seafood Bisque, 78
Sesame-Soy Barbecued Albacore, 40
Shad, 12-13, 36
Baked, 42
Roe
Baked in Cream, 42
Butter-Broiled, 42
Butter-Sautéed, 43
how to prepare, 42
Sheepshead, 51
Shell Macaroni with Clams, 92
Shellfish, 4-11, 56-94
abalone, 87-89, 93-94
Cioppino, 75
clams, 87-92
crab, 71-78
freezing, 11
lobster, 64-70
mussels, 87, 92-93
oysters, 79-83
scallops, 79-80, 84-86
shrimp, 57-63
Shrimp, 57-63
and Potato Salad, 62
Butterflied Appetizer, 58
Cocktail Sauce, 58
cooking directions, 57
Curried, 62
Hawaiian, 63
Deveining raw, 57-58
Dilled Shrimp-and-Cheese Rolls, 60, 61
Eggs Fried with Shrimp and Dill, 60
Fan-Tail, 62
Fried Balls, 59
Hot Prawn and Grapefruit Cocktail, 59
Hot with Dill Butter, 58
Iced in Dill Marinade, 58
-Oyster Creole, 83
Paella Valenciana, 62
Sauce, 29
Tetrazzini, 63
Toast Canapés
Tomato Slices with Shrimp Topping, 60
Simple cold fish sauces, 10-11
Small whole fish, 46-50
Smelt, 12-13, 46
Pickled Smelt Rolls, 48
Smoked
Barbecued Albacore, 39
Fish and Egg Bake, 41
Fish in Caper Cream Sauce, 41
how to steam, 28
sablefish, 35, 41
salmon, 28
Sole, 12-13, 14-19
à la Wickett, 18
and Crab Mousse, 18, 19
Filbert-Crusted, 15
Fillet Astoria, 15
Fillet Bonne Femme, 17
Grilled, 14
in Mushroom Sauce, 14
Kauai Fillet of, 16
Mushroom-Baked, 16
Oyster-Stuffed Florentine, 19
Pescado en Concha, 16
with Shallots in Cream, 17
Sportfish, 12-13, 51-56, 87-94
see also individual names of fish and shellfish
Steamed Clams in Wine Broth, 91
Striped Bass, 52
Baked with Cheese Crumb Topping, 56
Barbecued, 55
Cioppino, 56
Stuffed with Tomato Sauce, 56
with Carrot Stuffing, 56
Stuffed
Bonito with Tomatoes, 54
Mussels, 92
Striped Bass with Tomato Sauce, 56
Tomato Salads, 38
Sturgeon, 12-13, 36
Pan-Fried, 43
Pickled, 43
Surfperch, 12-13, 46-47
Butter Sautéed, 48
Swedish Salmon Bowl, 34
Swordfish, 12-13, 36
Baked, Manzanillo, 45
Barbecued with Basil-Garlic Baste, 44
Broiled, Sinaloa, 44
on Skewer, 45
Stroganoff, 45

Tarragon Butter- Sautéed Scallops, 86
Tartare Sauce, 10
Tomato Bearnaise Sauce, 70
Tomato Sauce, 9
Tomato Slices with Shrimp Topping, 60
Trout, 47
boning, 48
Brazilian Baked, 50
Butterflied and Barbecued, 48
Chilled with Dill Sauce, 50
in Butter Sauce, 49
Mushroom-Stuffed Baked, 49
Oven-Crisp, 50
Sautéed with Mushrooms in Cream, 50
Turkish Lobster Salad, 67

White seabass, 12-13, 21
Baked Whole, 27
Glazed Fillet of, 22
Sea Stew, 27
with Shrimp Sauce, 29

PHOTOGRAPHERS: Glenn M. Christiansen, pages 61, 74, 84; Darrow M. Watt, pages 19, 31, 44, 49, 69, 91